DATE DUE

JAN 31 1994	
DEC - 1 1994	
JAN 20 1995	
DEC - 3 199	
NOV 13 1998	
DEC 22 1999	

BRODART Cat. No. 23-221

The Radical Right and the Welfare State

Studies in international social policy and welfare

Series Editors: Professor Stewart MacPherson, University of Papua New Guinea
Professor James Midgley, Louisiana State University

Other titles available:

Comparative Social Policy and the Third World. Stewart MacPherson and James Midgley

The Welfare State in Capitalist Society: Policies of Retrenchment and Maintenance in Europe, North America and Australia. Ramesh Mishra

The Crisis in Welfare: An International Perspective on Social Services and Social Work. Brian Munday (editor)

Modern Welfare States: A Comparative View of Trends and Prospects. Robert Friedmann, Neil Gilbert and Moshe Sherer (editors)

The Radical Right and the Welfare State

An International Assessment

Edited by

Howard Glennerster and James Midgley

Harvester Wheatsheaf

Barnes & Noble Books

First published in Great Britain in 1991 by
Harvester Wheatsheaf
66 Wood Lane End, Hemel Hempstead
Hertfordshire, HP2 4RG
A division of
Simon & Schuster International Group

First published in the USA in 1991 by
Barnes & Noble Books
8705 Bollman Place
Savage, Maryland, 20763

Typeset in 10/12 pt Times
by MHL Typesetting Ltd, Coventry

Printed and bound in Great Britain by
Billings and Sons Limited, Worcester

British Library Cataloguing in Publication Data

The radical right and the welfare state:
An international assessment. — (Studies in international social policy and welfare)
I. Glennerstér, Howard II. Midgley, James
III. Series
361.2

ISBN 0-7450-0978-6

Library of Congress Cataloging-in-Publication Data

Available from the publisher

ISBN 0-389-20976-7

1 2 3 4 5 95 94 93 92 91

Contents

Contributors

Silvia Borzutzky is Assistant Professor, Department of Political Science, University of Pittsburgh. She holds doctoral degrees from the University of Pittsburgh and the School of Law, University of Chile. She has published numerous articles and book chapters on issues of social welfare in Chile and her book *The State, Politics and Social Security Policies in Chile* is due to be published by the University of Pittsburgh Press later this year.

Howard Glennerster is Professor of Social Administration at the London School of Economics. His books include *The Finance of Education* (Open University Press, 1971); *Social Service Budgets and Social Policy* (Allen and Unwin, 1975); *The Future of the Welfare State* (Heinemann, 1983); and *Paying for Welfare* (Blackwell, 1985).

Howard Jacob Karger is Associate Professor, School of Social Work, Louisiana State University. He formerly taught at the University of Missouri, Columbia. His books include *Sentinels of Order* (University Press of America, 1987), *Social Workers and Labor Unions* (Greenwood Press, 1988) and (with David Stoesz) *American Social Welfare Policy* (Longman, 1990).

Ernie Lightman is Professor of Social Work at the School of Social Work, University of Toronto. He has written extensively on issues of social policy in Canada and the United Kingdom where he taught at the London School of Economics for a period.

Steen Mangen is Lecturer in Social Administration at the London School of Economics with special reference to European social policy. He has published widely in this field of European social policy.

James Midgley is Professor of Social Work and Dean of the School of Social Work at Louisiana State University. He has published *Professional Imperialism: Social Work in the Third World* (Heinemann, 1981); *The Social Dimensions of Development* (Wiley, 1982) (with Margaret Hardiman); *Social Security, Inequality and the Third World* (Wiley, 1984); *Community Participation, Social Development and the State* (Methuen, 1986); and *Comparative Social Policy and the Third World* (Harvester Wheatsheaf, 1987) (with Stewart MacPherson). He is co-editor (with Stewart MacPherson) of a series entitled *Studies in International Social Policy and Welfare*, which is published by Harvester Wheatsheaf.

Menachem Monnickendam teaches social work at Bar-Ilan University in Israel. He is a consultant on mental health and has published extensively on social work research methods.

David Stoesz is Associate Professor of Social Work at San Diego State University. He is the co-author of *American Social Welfare Policy* (Longman, 1990) (with Howard Karger) and the author of numerous articles on issues of social policy which have been published in the leading journals in the social welfare field including *Social Service Review*, *Social Work*, *Social Development Issues*, *Administration in Social Work* and *Journal of Sociology and Social Work*.

Preface

The welfare state has been a distinguishing feature of social life in the twentieth century. For much of the century, governments throughout the world have accepted the principle of state responsibility for the welfare of citizens. This has resulted in the introduction of state-sponsored social security, health care, education, housing, social work and other human service programmes in both the industrial and developing countries. Although there are significant differences in the degree to which governments have allocated resources to the social services, or have managed to meet the needs of their citizens, state involvement in welfare has been ubiquitous and internationally accepted. Despite ideological differences between various political parties and governments, thinking about social welfare during the post-war era was dominated by what has been described as a 'welfare consensus', forged by the supporters of both the political right and left, which institutionalized the idea of government intervention in social affairs.

During the 1980s, the welfare consensus was severely shaken by radical right-wing political leaders who popularized the idea that state-sponsored welfare is inimical to national well-being and to economic and social progress. These leaders drew political support from disaffected elements within the established conservative movement who had come to believe that economic growth, cherished traditional values, established beliefs and national pride had been undermined by the insidious spread and docile acceptance of socialist ideas during the post-war era. Economic stagnation, trade union militancy, rampant inflation, the apparent decline in patriotism, the unruliness of the young, the pace of moral and social change and other ills were all regarded as symptomatic of this deeper malaise. The unwillingness of centrist liberals and conventional conservatives to oppose socialism and halt the decline of traditional society enraged the radical right and fostered their mobilization and resolve. Skilfully exploiting economic difficulties and popular beliefs and fears, they scored notable electoral successes in several countries and sought, through various policy initiatives, to undermine the tradition of centrist consensus politics that had characterized the preceding decades. The welfare state was high on their agenda of socialist inspired institutions listed for destruction.

The rise of the radical right during the 1970s and 1980s has been extensively documented in Britain and the United States where the movement's ideas were (with the exception of Chile) perhaps most vigorously implemented. Designated variously as *New Right*, *neo-liberal* or *neo-conservative*, the politics associated with Mrs Thatcher in England and with President Reagan in the United States have formed the basis for various scholarly accounts which have described the economic and social policies adopted by these administrations and assessed their consequences. However, no attempt has previously been made to offer a comprehensive international assessment of the radical right and its impact on the welfare state.

Although the movement's ideas were extensively implemented in the policies of the Thatcher and Reagan administrations, they also found expression in other European countries, and in several developing countries as well. The case of Chile under the Pinochet regime is perhaps the best publicized of attempts by radical right-wing leaders to reverse the tendency towards welfarism in the developing world, but other Third World governments (particularly in Latin America) have also been affected by radical right-wing ideology. In addition, radical right-wing thinking has had considerable influence in international agencies such as the International Monetary Fund (IMF) and to a lesser extent the World Bank. Through their lending policies, these agencies have been able to compel many heavily indebted developing countries to implement adjustment policies which reflect radical right economic thinking, and which have had serious consequences for the social services of these nations.

The 1980s may legitimately be described as the decade of the radical right, since it was during this period that the movement gained political ascendancy and was able to implement many of its policies. By the end of the decade, however, there was a sense that the ideological force of radical right-wing ideas had been spent. Terms that had been popular at the beginning of the 1980s, such as *New Right* and *neo-conservative* had largely fallen into disuse and compared to the early 1980s, the economic doctrines of monetarism and supply side economics were being infrequently mentioned. Reinforcing the perception of the decline of the radical right was the fading from public prominence of political leaders who had implemented their policies with a distinctly combative determination during the 1980s. At the end of the decade, Mr Reagan completed two terms as President of the United States and was succeeded by an administration which not only failed to recite the dogmas of *New Right* ideology, but popularized notions of a 'kinder, gentler America'. In the closing months of 1990, Mrs Thatcher resigned as Prime Minister of the United Kingdom still clinging tenaciously to her beliefs in the face of obvious opposition from her colleagues and a sizeable proportion of the electorate. Under pressure from the United States, and faced with significant electoral antipathy to his leadership and policies, General Pinochet retired to the barracks. While still firmly in control of the institutions of state power, the General no longer commands the attention he previously enjoyed.

Now that the 1980s are over, it is appropriate that an assessment of the impact of radical right-wing thinking on the social services and the welfare state be undertaken. In various countries, but particularly in Britain and the United States, radical policy measures which challenged the centrist consensus and the welfare state were enthusiastically adopted. These measures have had negative consequences for the welfare state ideal, but the extent to which they have significantly altered institutionalized approaches to governmental welfare provision is debatable. While some believe that the welfare state has been severely damaged as a result of the implementation of radical right-wing policies, others are of the opinion that only minor modifications have been introduced. There are differences of opinion also about the effects of these policies on the well-being of ordinary people. While some conclude that needy groups in the population have experienced a sharp decline in incomes and standards of living as a result of cuts in social expenditures, others believe that levels of welfare have not been greatly affected. There are also some who believe that standards of living have in fact improved.

Since there are significant differences between the different countries in which the radical right exercised power, the effects of these ideas should be examined within a wider international context. Much of the existing literature on the radical right deals almost exclusively with Britain and the United States, and little attention has been given to the impact of these ideas in other societies. By examining the movement's ideology and policies in different societies, the book offers a unique, internationally focused account of the radical right and its implications for the welfare state.

It may, of course, be argued that since the leading proponents of the radical right are no longer in office, an assessment of this kind is superfluous. Indeed, the declining use of terms such as *New Right*, and the apparent demise of the enthusiasm with which the movement's ideas were implemented in the 1980s, may suggest that the movement is now a vestige of the past. But, as various contributors to this book will demonstrate, the radical right's influence has not dissipated. In countries where its policy prescriptions were embraced, they remain intact in spite of the popularization of new slogans which ostensibly contradict the vigour and determination of the movement's original agenda. In these countries also, there is a need for an assessment of the impact on people's welfare of the policies that radical right-wing leaders implemented. An account of this kind is not only required for purposes of historical documentation, but for a normative assessment of the effects of the movement's social policies on social well-being in different parts of the world.

As is the case with most writing on contemporary political movements, the literature on the radical right has not produced a standardized terminology. As was suggested earlier, a variety of synonyms including *New Right*, neo-conservatism, neo-liberalism, libertarianism and radical individualism have been used by different writers at different times. Often, these terms emphasize one aspect of radical right-wing thinking and fail to capture its wider connotation. The issue is further complicated by the use of different terminologies in different societies. In spite of the current popularity of the term *neo-conservative*, it has a rather different and more precise connotation in the United States where, as is shown in the first chapter of the book, the neo-conservatives are a group of intellectuals who emphasize the traditionalist elements in conventional conservative thought rather than the radical economic individualism which has characterized the writings of many radical right-wing thinkers. In the United States also, the term *New Right* has a distinct association with populist, traditionalist elements among the radical right and this meaning differs significantly from the British usage where the term has been used in a more generic sense to refer to the radical right in general. The term 'neo-liberal' is sometimes also used as a synonym and particularly for the economic individualist elements in radical right-wing ideology. The term is also quite popular in Latin America and Europe. But here again, it has also been used to refer to American liberals who seek to reconstruct the centrist liberal agenda to fit the new realities of the age. Neo-liberals oppose right-wing doctrines but they also criticize statist New Dealers for advocating outmoded approaches to social and economic policy. Theirs is a more pragmatic approach which lays less emphasis on state interventionism and advocates the institutionalization of both economic and welfare pluralism. Their work is significant for offering a revisionist agenda for mainstream American liberalism.

No attempt will be made to standardize or analyze the various terms which have been used with reference to the radical right. Since this book is not intended to examine questions of political science nomenclature, a lengthy discussion of terminology is beyond its proper scope. Nevertheless, some references to these different usages will be made in the first chapter which seeks to provide an orientation to the disparate elements in radical right-wing ideology. However, no attempt has been made to standardize usages in the other chapters where the authors have sometimes varied the terminologies to fit their own preferences.

The nature of this book

In its examination of radical right-wing ideas and their effects on social policy in an international context, the book is organized in three parts which seek respectively to provide a conceptual background to the subject, to examine the impact of radical right ideas in different countries, and to draw general conclusions.

Part I of the book traces the historical development of the radical right as a political movement and describes the social, economic and political notions which comprise its ideology. It also discusses the implications of radical right-wing ideas for the welfare state, paying particular attention to proposals for altering existing welfare state programmes through privatization, the expansion of voluntary and non-formal effort and other measures. This part of the book focuses largely on Britain and the United States. This is not only because of the extensive documentation of radical right policies and programmes in these countries, but because it is in here that the radical right's agenda has been so vigorously implemented.

Part II of the book consists of country case studies. Some of these focus on particular facets of state welfare provision, such as income maintenance or health care, so that implications for particular social services can be examined in more depth. Others are more broadly focused, reviewing the impact of radical right-wing ideas on domestic social policies in general. The case studies are drawn from countries in different regions of the world, and offer insights into the ways radical right-wing ideas have found expression in different economic, social and cultural settings. In addition to articles on Britain and the United States, case study material from Chile, Canada, Germany and Israel is included. Much of this material is new and departs significantly from established approaches in comparative social policy research, which often provide descriptive catalogues of human service provision rather than analytical or normative commentary. By focusing on radical right-wing policies on existing state welfare programmes, the authors transcend description and offer useful insights into the role of ideology in social policy.

Part III of the book consists of one concluding chapter which reviews the country case studies in Part II and asks what impact the radical right has had on the welfare state. Have the changes that have been introduced permanently altered the welfare state and entrenched new approaches to social need, or have they resulted in little more than marginal modifications? The chapter also considers the future of the welfare state in the light of radical right-wing policies and programmes. Will new conservative administrations continue to have electoral appeal and if so, will they perpetuate radical right-wing antipathies to the welfare state? Will alternative governments come to power and reinstate the welfare consensus? By seeking to answer these and other questions, the chapter draws the book's contents together into a comprehensive, concluding commentary.

The authors of the various chapters are recognized authorities on social policy and on the countries they describe. A list of the contributors together with relevant biographic detail is provided at the beginning of the book. The editors are indebted to them for their willingness to collaborate in this study. They would like to thank the OECD for permission to reproduce tables from *Aging Populations: Social Policy Implications* (Paris, 1988) in Chapter 9, and also Child Poverty Action Group for permission to reproduce table 26 from *Poverty: The Facts* by Carey Oppenheim (CPAG Ltd, 1990) in the same chapter. They also acknowledge, with gratitude, the support of Clare Grist, publishing editor at Harvester Wheatsheaf. She has been patient, encouraging and helpful.

Howard Glennerster
London School of Economics

James Midgley
Louisiana State University

Part I

Theories, policies and prescriptions

1

The radical right, politics and society

James Midgley

It is very difficult to offer precise definitions of those constellations of ideas, beliefs and prescriptions for political action that are called ideologies. If commonplace terms such as 'socialism', 'liberalism' and 'conservatism' are interpreted in varying ways, expressions for the radical right such as *New Right* or *neo-conservative* are not likely to be subjected to unambiguous definition. In spite of the growth of a substantive literature on the subject, a standard definition of the radical right remains elusive. Although various social scientists have documented the movement's activities, and shown that the term has an essential validity, they have not been able to encapsulate its diverse ideological themes, political manifestations and social ramifications within one, all-encompassing statement.

The ideas comprising radical right ideology are complex, multi-faceted and even internally inconsistent. Several authorities have drawn attention to the apparent contradictory beliefs held by leaders such as Mrs Thatcher whose radical commitment to economic individualism coexists (with apparent ease) with her social and cultural traditionalism, and authoritarian leadership style. Similarly, while the radical right forms a part of the conservative movement, it has been distinguished not by its defence of the status quo, but by its challenge to the institutionalization of centrist consensus politics which has characterized the post-war era. An inconsistency is revealed also in Hayek's insistence that he is not a conservative, even though he is universally acclaimed as one of the movement's most influential mentors (Hayek, 1960).

Despite these apparent contradictions, most authorities agree that the diverse ideological threads of radical right-wing thinking have been intertwined to weave a coherent corpus of ideas, beliefs and policy prescriptions. This chapter will attempt a brief overview of these ideologies with particular reference to the major historical events which gave rise to the radical right, and which led ultimately to its coming to power during the 1980s. Its purpose is to offer a broad introduction to the collection, and to provide an orientation to the more focused accounts in the remainder of this book that seek to examine the impact of radical right-wing ideas on the welfare state in different parts of the world.

The notion of the radical right

It is not certain where the terms such as *New Right* and *neo-conservative* originated, but their use in connection with the Reagan and Thatcher administrations in the 1980s has ensured their historical perpetuity. As was noted in the preface to this book, the 1980s may legitimately be described as the decade of the radical right, since it was during these years that the movement attracted widespread electoral support, secured political power in Britain and the United States, and began to exert considerable international influence.

Several academic analyses of the radical right have now been published, and these have offered helpful accounts of the movement's historical origins, ideological commitments and political successes. However, these accounts tend to emphasize specific facets of radical right ideology, and they frequently deal exclusively with developments in only one country. For example, Bosanquet's (1983) pioneering study is primarily concerned with events in Britain, and stresses the radical economic individualism in Mrs Thatcher's administration, which is derived from the writings of Hayek and Friedman. In their review of late twentieth-century conservatism, Gottfried and Fleming (1988) focus exclusively on developments in the United States, and define the radical right as a populist phenomenon; elements of economic libertarianism and social traditionalism are not subsumed under the movement and are treated as separate categories. Other authors have stressed the authoritarian tendencies of the radical right, its flirtation with nationalist (and racist) ideas (Seidel, 1986), and its association with Christian fundamentalism (Bruce, 1988; Diamond, 1989).

Some commentators do not define the radical right primarily in ideological terms, but focus instead on the movement's political techniques and statecraft. Riddell argues, for example, that 'Thatcherism is essentially an . . . approach to leadership rather than an ideology' (Riddell, 1983, p. 7). These accounts also de-emphasize the appeal of ideology in the radical right's electoral success. Instead, they stress the abilities of radical right leaders to cope with the political and economic realities of the 1970s by adroitly extricating themselves from the corporatist leanings of previous administrations. It was this manoeuvring which offered an electorally appealing alternative to conventional political problem-solving approaches; while Mr Heath and his Labour successors in Britain tried unsuccessfully to establish a workable corporatist strategy for controlling inflation, Mrs Thatcher won electoral support by castigating state intervention as the cause of societal discontent (Bulpitt, 1986). Explanations of the motivation of the radical right's statecraft also vary. While Riddell (1983) views the movement's electoral efforts as essentially pragmatic, Hall (1983; 1985) sees them as conspiratorially manipulative; the radical right, he argues, is engaged in a 'hegemonic project' which fosters authoritarian populism in an attempt to impose its world view on society.

By defining the radical right as a political movement, other commentators have also de-emphasized ideology. Gottfried and Fleming (1988) have shown that the radical right's electoral success has been secured through an effective populist appeal to grass roots sentiment, often in direct association with established social, moral and religious movements. These 'general purpose political organizations' are, they suggest, not driven as much by ideology as by an internal organizational impetus fuelled by a sense of discontent and alienation. Viguerie, Weyrich, Phillips and other leaders of popular conservative organizations in the United States are campaigners rather than ideologues. Indeed, Viguerie's (1981) own account of his movement's agenda lays more stress on tactics than ideologically defined goals. A concern with tactics also characterized the close links which were forged between the secular right and the fundamentalist New Christian Right during the early 1980s. Religious fundamentalists seldom engaged in intellectual discourse on ideological issues, but were more inclined to support the radical right leadership because of its commitment to social traditionalism and pietism (Bruce, 1988).

Although concepts such as 'movement' and 'statecraft' are helpful in offering an account of the radical right, the issue of ideology cannot be avoided. The effective mobilization of mass movements requires causes, and causes are usually defined and shaped by ideological beliefs. Indeed, the effective manipulation of popular sentiment is, in its own right, an expression of beliefs about the significance of 'the people' and the 'popular will' in the political process (Canovan, 1981). Nor can the effective exercise of statecraft be readily distinguished from ideological considerations. Since the legitimation of power requires justification on ideological grounds, the ability to manipulate the political process is seldom devoid of ideological significance.

The empirical evidence also contradicts the views of those commentators who have de-emphasized the notion of ideology in their accounts of the radical right. Mr Reagan and Mrs Thatcher's homespun pronouncements are not ideologically vacuous but reflective of deeply held beliefs. Their association with organizations such as the Institute for Economic Affairs and the Centre for Policy Studies in Britain, and the American Enterprise Institute, the Hoover Institution and the Heritage Foundation in the United States, also belies the suggestion that ideology is not of primary significance in explaining the radical right's political success. Although it is true that the radical right has no simple ideology, it forged a unique blend of political beliefs to create a coherent and appealing agenda for action.

In examining the idea of the radical right, the notion of 'the Old Right' is invariably raised. But while the ideology of the radical right stands in an antonymous relationship with the ideology of established conservatism, few commentators have been able to differentiate clearly between the essential elements of radical and conventional right thinking. In the United States, where Old Right supporters are somewhat unkindly known as paleoconservatives, the differences are often ascribed to bitter personality clashes rather than to major differences in ideological persuasion (Gottfried and Fleming, 1988). Nevertheless, it is possible, as Judis (1990a) claims, to identify in the paleoconservative approach a return to pre-war isolationism, economic protectionism, and outmoded beliefs about Soviet expansionism and the threat of global communism.

In Britain, personality differences between radical and old right factions are no less bitter. *New Right* journalists delight in ridiculing Old Right conservatives as the 'grouse brigade . . . distinguished for their wealth, wetness and country pursuits' (Levitas, 1986, p. 9). Although the radical right successfully challenged the rural squirearchy's control over party affairs and, in so doing, reflected the ascendancy of *nouveau riche* elements within the Conservative party, the polarization of New and Old Right beliefs cannot be attributed only to class origins. While Mr Pym may have exemplified the influence of aristocratic elements within established conservatism, Mr Heath's social background mirrors that of Mrs Thatcher.

Intolerance and brashness of political style have also distinguished the New from the Old Right. The radical right adopted tactics which diverged markedly from the traditional gentility of old-fashioned conservative politics. Radical right adherents also flaunted a callous attitude towards the needy and underprivileged which diverged from official Tory pronouncements. They virulently attacked establishment political figures, and declared their contempt for institutionalized centrist policies, such as economic management and welfarism. This appalled many traditional conservatives, who reacted by rallying in support of popular social programmes such as the National Health Service. But while the welfarist concerns of conservative 'wets' in Britain, and President Bush's notions of a 'kinder and gentler' America contrast starkly with the cultivated toughness of both Mr Reagan and Mrs Thatcher, they do not tell the full story; radicalism was undoubtedly a relevant factor, but more significant was an underlying discontent with the Old Right's conventional policy approaches. The institutionalization of the welfare state, economic planning and other 'left-leaning' ideas with the support of establishment conservatism infuriated those right-wing factions that later emerged as the *radical right*. It also galvanized their resolve to break the centrist mould which had shaped post-war politics.

Established Toryism in Britain has, as Moran (1985) pointed out, long managed to encompass a variety of beliefs pragmatically, and it is this pragmatic tradition that led conservatives to accept the idea of the welfare state, and to participate in the creation of the so-called post-war liberal consensus. Macmillan personified this approach. Loney (1986, p. 2) quotes one of his speeches which explicated the centrist position: the Conservative Party, he argued, opposes both collectivism with its denial of individual rights and responsibilities and '*laissez-faire* individualism' which abrogates the notion of community and reciprocal helping. As he put it: 'We stand . . . to block the way to both these extremes and to all such extremes, and to point the path towards moderate and balanced views.'

The radical right's distinctive agenda lay in its determination to destroy the liberal consensus. The radical *New Right* faction challenged ꝛight and enthusiastically embraced ideas that complemented ːion of establishment consensus politics. The initial, and most ɹl of these ideas was economic individualism. Advocating a return ιο a supposedly pure *laissez-faire* past, the radical right offered a new and electorally appealing alternative to government management in countries where corporatist strategies had failed to pacify trade union demands, revive economic growth and control rampant inflation. Other ideological themes were also incorporated into the radical right's political odyssey. Populist sentiments were dextrously manipulated not merely for electoral advantage, but because the radical right leadership earnestly believed in them. While the Falklands affair, and the invasion of Grenada brought considerable electoral benefit, both Mrs Thatcher and Mr Reagan took genuine pride in the nationalist sentiments these events engendered. By extolling the virtues of strong leadership, the radical right's populism also revealed an authoritarian tendency which some found disturbing because of its reminiscence of the dictatorships that only a generation earlier had effectively harnessed populist ideas to the fascist cause. Notions of cultural and social traditionalism were also pursued by the radical right. Apart from their populist appeal, the advocacy of traditionalism was an attempt to reaffirm dearly held values that radical right leaders believe were under attack by left-leaning intellectuals, the 1960s counterculture and modern day misguided youth.

The three ideological themes of economic individualism, cultural traditionalism and authoritarian populism are at the centre of the radical right's world view. They permeated the processes which led to the movement's emergence in the 1980s as a highly organized and powerful political force with a formidable agenda for action.

The problem of statism and the promise of economic freedom

The rapid expansion of state interventionism into social and economic affairs during the twentieth century has been unprecedented. While many examples of intrusive authoritarian states can be found throughout history, the proactive involvement of government in the planning and management of the modern economy, in meeting social needs, in providing utilities and other services, and in engaging in economic production has no historical parallel. Inspired by various collectivist ideologies, statism became ascendant in the industrial countries during the latter part of the nineteenth century, and achieved general acceptance after the Second World War. Although the state had often been viewed as an agent of tyranny, corruption and other ills, a new conception of the state as responsible, benevolent and protective gained acceptance.

The institutionalization of statism was the consequence not only of the appeal of socialist ideology, but of political pressure from an enfranchised populace which came to expect that social and economic problems would be ameliorated through government action. The idea that society had inherent mechanisms for automatically correcting economic and social dysfunctions lost popularity during the Great Depression. The inability of the market economy to respond to the crisis of the depression and of established institutions such as the family, church and community to care for those in need, stimulated demand for comprehensive programmes which would protect the population as a whole against social and economic adversity. While the welfare state embodied the ideal of the caring society, Keynesian economics offered the prospect of preventing similar catastrophes in the future. And it was this hope that led to the acceptance of interventionist strategies by both centrist liberals and traditional conservatives. The failure of the market to solve the economic crisis of the 1930s required alternative prescriptions which were previously regarded as ideologically unpalatable.

Opposition to statist interventionism in the Western industrial nations during the decades following the Second World War was limited. McCarthy's strident anti-communism in the United States, and the warnings of libertarian economists such as Hayek (1944), and writers such as Harris and Seldon (1965) at the Institute for Economic Affairs in Britain, failed to stem the heady expansion of statist enterprise during the 1950s. By the 1960s, both right- and left-leaning political parties had endorsed statism, and accepted the idea that public agencies should manage the economy, regulate commercial and industrial activities, subsidize incomes, provide a wide range of human services, manage sizeable social security funds and even own and operate large industrial enterprises. The steady rise in levels of living, and a pervasive sense of well-being contrasted sharply with social conditions just a generation earlier. In this climate, politics converged to create what has been described as the post-war liberal consensus (Bell, 1960; Kerr *et al.*, 1973). As the major political parties in both Europe and

North America competed on a limited ideological field for electoral support, the political influence of radical movements further on the right and left declined. And, in the electoral campaigns of the time, the continued expansion of public services became a central feature of political platforms. By the 1970s, public expenditures had reached unprecedented proportions, and although some doomsayers were warning of the dangers of 'government overload' (King, 1975; Crozier *et al.*, 1975), statist expansionism continued apace.

By the mid-1970s, however, post-war prosperity was under threat. The oil crisis, stagnant economic growth, increased labour activism, inflation, capital flight, deindustrialization, falling productivity, and other economic problems were impeding the ability of governments to satisfy rising expectations, and deal effectively with the problems of the day. In some European countries such as Austria, the post-war liberal consensus was transformed into a highly structured corporatist arrangement by which labour, industry and the state forged compacts that mediated political pressures. In others, such as Britain and the United States, the corporatist strategy failed in spite of the attempts of various political parties to reach accord with dominant constituencies (Smith, 1979; Schmitter and Lembruch, 1979).

It was in this economic climate that the radical right emerged as a serious political force within the established conservative movement. Espousing libertarian economic ideas which advocated a minimalist state, and urging a return to the pure market, the radical right successfully defined the state not as the solution but as the cause of society's problems. The electoral appeal of this slogan must be seen in the context of popular frustration about the failure of previous centrist governments to forge a corporatist compact and to deal effectively with economic and social ills through statist mechanisms. Also of importance was the combination of the libertarian message with populist electoral techniques such as the promise of lower taxation.

Radical right leaders drew extensively on economic individualism to develop programmes for managing the economy and social affairs. Although Hayek, Schumpeter, Friedman and others provided the theories within which the specific policy formulations of monetarism and supply-side economics were developed, the movement drew greater inspiration from the wider individualist philosophies undergirding the technical prescriptions of these doctrines. Also relevant were the writings of Nozick (1974) and other anarcho-individualists whose antipathies to statism found expression not in conventional anarchist communitarian prescriptions, but in the advocacy of an extreme atomistic individualism. And, although public declarations of loyalty to monetarism and supply-side economics waned, the influence of these wider individualist ideas persisted.

A variety of themes characterized the critique of state interventionism. Although the lessons of the Great Depression had convinced an earlier generation of conservatives of the need for state economic management, the radical right exploited the economic problems of the 1970s to argue effectively for a return to the free market. They claimed that the institutionalization of the market free of state regulation was the only solution to economic ills. The pursuit of full employment was an illusion, East European communism had demonstrated the failure of the command economy to satisfy wants and expectations, and governments had become bloated with inefficiency and wastage. In this regard, the writings of Buchanan and Tullock (1962), Niskanen (1971; 1973) and other 'public choice' theorists offered an appealing critique of the bureaucracy as self-interested and self-perpetuating. The only prospect of curtailing statist wastage is to reduce the monopolistic powers of government agencies, and to subject bureaucratic management to competition.

Economic individualism was manifested in various radical right policies. Firstly, both Mrs Thatcher and Mr Reagan's administrations used monetarism and supply-side economics to justify substantial cuts in public expenditures and, at the same time, to cut levels of taxation, particularly for higher income earners. Both also justified the exponential increase in the discount rate in terms of these theories. But, as King (1987) observed, the aggregate size of the public sector did not decrease during the 1980s and instead, budgetary policy resulted in a significant shift in existing allocations from social to military and law enforcement expenditures. The failure to reduce public spending in either Britain or the United States was in part due to increased pressures on the public sector resulting from the economic recession and increased unemployment induced by monetarist principles (Ashton, 1989), but it was also a reflection of the ideological priorities of radical right governments which increased budgetary allocations for defence and other programmes that were compatible with its traditionalist and populist agenda.

A second aspect of the radical right's economic individualism relates to taxation. Radical right governments not only advocated cuts in taxation in order to stimulate entrepreneurship and individual initiative but implemented tax cuts once they assumed office. The theoretical basis for tax cuts have been explicated by the supply-side school which has claimed, with the help of econometric models, that current levels of taxation in the industrial economies create disincentives, stifle investment, reduce economic output and thus diminish tax revenues. Supply-siders argue, therefore, that if governments wish to increase the flow of tax revenues, they need to lower current levels of taxation. A variation on this idea is that current levels of taxation in the industrial countries are so high that commercial enterprises and entrepreneurs are compelled to engage in increasingly complex and sophisticated forms of tax avoidance. Lower levels of taxation would induce corporations and wealthy individuals to pay taxes rather than avoid or evade them.

Radical right governments have used these arguments to legitimize significant tax cuts for those in higher income brackets. Although these cuts were ostensibly intended to benefit the community as a whole, analyses of the beneficiaries of the 1981 Kemp–Roth tax cuts in the United States found that 85 per cent of the benefits accrued to taxpayers earning more than $50,000 per annum (Leckachmen, 1982). In Britain, where similar cuts were introduced, Loney (1986) reported that the top 1 per cent of taxpayers received 44 per cent of the £4 billion released by the government while the poorest 25 per cent received only 3 per cent of this amount. A more recent American analysis (Phillips, 1990) has concluded that the 1980s produced a massive redistribution of income in favour of the wealthy. While the average after-tax incomes of the nation's wealthiest families increased from about $190,000 in the late 1970s to about $400,000 in the late 1980s, families earning less than $16,000 experienced a decline of about 10 per cent in their incomes. Middle income families have also suffered a decline in their average incomes of about 7 per cent. Although tax cuts have undoubtedly benefited high income earners, they have not had a magical effect on the economy. Contrary to the supply-siders' predictions, investment declined from 6.9 per cent as a share of gross national product (GNP) in 1979 to 5.0 per cent in 1988, and the economic growth rate of 2.5 per cent in 1988 was slightly lower than the growth rate of 2.6 per cent in 1979 (Kotz, 1989). The problem has been exacerbated by the loss of revenues to the Federal government which now has a deficit of mammoth proportions.

A third expression of the radical right's economic individualism is deregulation, and the denationalization of public enterprises. Both approaches enjoyed popular support in the early 1980s, and enhanced the movement's credibility. After coming to office, the Thatcher government denationalized a substantial number of enterprises which previous Labour governments had regarded as integral to their socialist commitment, and which previous Conservative governments had retained. Particularly controversial was the denationalization of public utilities such as British Gas and British Telecom, both of which were profitable and brought significant revenues into the Treasury. In the United States, the deregulation of airlines, broadcasting, oil and gas, railways and telecommunications paralleled the radical move towards denationalization in Britain. Here, as in Britain, deregulation has not ended the trend towards monopolization: instead of freeing market forces, mergers and takeovers have been a distinctive feature of the New Right era, further concentrating economic power.

Closely associated with the move towards denationalization and deregulation is the radical right's determination to end the power of the trade unions. Although libertarian thinkers such as Hayek recognize the role of unions in a free, competitive economic order, opposition to the unions has been justified on grounds of excess and the alleged thwarting of the productive process (Hayek, 1960; 1978). The legitimation of various legislative measures designed to curtail trade union activities in Britain was secured by the failure of the coal miners to oppose the Thatcherite offensive. Long regarded as the shock troops of the labour movement, the miners were unable to repeat the successes they had scored against Mr Heath in the mid-1970s. In the United States, the air traffic controllers suffered a similar defeat in their engagement with Mr Reagan.

A fourth element of radical right economic individualism involves the privatization of the social services. The reductions in social expenditures which occurred in various Western countries under radical right-wing governments in the 1980s were accompanied by deliberate policy inducements to private individuals, small businesses and large corporations to offer social services to citizens on a profit basis. As Stoesz (1986) has shown, these inducements have facilitated the emergence of a substantial 'corporate welfare sector' in the United

States. In Britain, where the commercial welfare sector remains small, the privatization of public housing represents a major achievement in the radical right's anti-welfarist programme.

The decline of civilization and the reconstruction of order

Conservatives have always valued tradition and order and, in the Burkian sense of the word, have sought to resist changes to established institutions and values. But, as was shown earlier, mainstream conservatism pragmatically accepted the expansion of statism and the rise of welfarism during the post-war era, adopting the view that the modern welfare state was an integral element of an advanced industrial society. More subtly, many conservatives also adjusted to changing post-war mores. Although some reacted with alarm to the new fads of the young, most accepted the youth culture of the 1950s with good-natured indulgence.

The rise of the counter-culture of the 1960s was a different matter. The venomous determination of campus revolutionaries, mass opposition to the Vietnam War, the militancy of trade unions, the popularization of drugs, the decline of religion, and the frequency of urban riots outraged conservatives who believed that these events threatened the survival of established society. Although the Johnson and Wilson administrations were hardly subversive of establishment values, they were increasingly associated with the permissiveness of the age, and it was perhaps inevitable that their electorate support would fade, though this was not apparent until the late 1960s. In Britain, where the Labour government had won a slender victory in the 1964 election, its majority was increased in 1966. And in the United States, Goldwater's showing in the 1964 presidential election suggested that his traditionalist conservatism was premature. By the end of the decade, however, as disaffection with social change and perceived instability became more widespread, conservative politicians were again in power in both Britain and the United States.

Conservative governments in these countries raised the expectations of their supporters that the forces of rampant modernism would be contained. Frank Meyer, a leading traditionalist conservative thinker, commended Mr Nixon in messianic terms as the country's best hope for dealing with the 'civilization crisis' of the time, and for being able to 'turn the tide of anarchy that threatens to engulf us' (Meye 1968, p. 859). In Britain, Mr Heath was not seen primarily as a defender of traditional cultural values, but as the best prospect for curbing the power of the trade unions. Mr Wilson and his government had established an uneasy compact with the unions and, as industrial action became more common, the conservative promise of restraining the labour movement was appealing.

Both politicians failed to meet these expectations, and both lost power in circumstances that contrasted ironically with their initial efforts to restore traditional order. Mr Heath was unable to contain labour unrest and he eventually succumbed in a major industrial conflagration. The Watergate affair dismayed Americans whose belief in the sanctity of traditional political institutions was fundamentally shaken; instead of upholding traditional authority, Watergate revealed that the presidency could be used to undermine cherished institutions. By the mid-1970s, centrist governments which supported corporatist strategies, were again in power.

These events were significant in the emergence of the radical right. Previous conservative governments were not perceived merely as having failed, but as somehow having betrayed the conservative cause. With Mrs Thatcher's election as leader of the British Conservative Party, Mr Heath was virtually outcasted. Similar sentiments were expressed against President Ford and Mr Rockefeller, who were seen by traditionalists as weak appeasers of liberal opinion. The failure of establishment conservatives to secure and exercise power decisively in favour of traditionalist causes engendered a radical backlash. It was in this climate that Viguerie and other electoral campaigners began to build coalitions around Mr Reagan who, it was generally believed, would implement the longed for traditionalist ideals that Goldwater had first espoused in his unsuccessful presidential campaign (Rusher, 1984).

The intellectual basis for conservative traditionalism can, of course, be traced back to Burke but, in more recent times, it is the writings of Kirk, Meyer and a revisionist group of scholars known as the neo-conservatives who have informed traditionalists within the movement. Kirk's (1953) seminal contribution lay in his reiteration of Burke's conception of the social order as an organic sharing of cultural beliefs between a people of common identity. These beliefs have a powerful binding quality that transcends generations. Although the neo-conservative restatement of traditionalism had a theological connotation that anticipated, in some respects, later collaborative efforts between secular radical right campaigners and the fundamentalist Christian movement, they were not explicated in religious terms. A conception of this kind would have been antithetical to the neo-conservative's academic origins but they, nevertheless, had a mystical quality which intensified the celebration of traditional American values.

Neo-conservatives also offered a critique of radical individualism which they regarded as a cause of the demise of self-discipline, order and respect for authority that characterized the age of the counter-culture. As Kristol (1978) pointed out, the relentless pursuit of self-interest may unleash powerful economic forces, but it also undermines the social order and its legitimacy. This rejection of radical individualism does not, of course, suggest that American neo-conservatives deny the centrality of individualism in conservative thought. Indeed, individualism is extolled for being a historical ingredient of the American experience. But radical individualism, and particularly those libertarian elements in radical individualism that license the free expression of individual preferences, are regarded as antithetical to the social and cultural order and are rejected. Similar ideas have been expressed in Britain by Scruton (1980) and other members of the neo-conservative Salisbury Group.

In spite of the neo-conservative critique of radical individualism, the radical right has adopted and managed to synthesize traditionalist with libertarian economic themes. Radical right-wing political leaders have, to some extent, drawn on the work of Kirk, Meyer and other fusionist thinkers who tackled the apparent contradiction between individualist and traditionalist ideas by stressing the historical compatibility of individualist and traditionalist beliefs. But perhaps the most effective device in this synthesis was the common denigration of statism by both traditionalist and libertarian thinkers; since the expansion of the state and the rise of welfarism is ahistorical and fundamentally alien to the Western experience, common ground between the two approaches can be found. A similar argument has been employed by writers of the fundamentalist New Christian Right in their critique of the welfare state (Midgley, 1990).

Radical right-wing political leaders have lost few opportunities to exploit popular disquiet about the apparent collapse of the social order. Mrs Thatcher often attributed current social ills to the permissiveness of earlier times. Edgar documents one speech in which Mrs Thatcher claimed: 'We are reaping what was sown in the 1960s [when] fashionable theories and permissive claptrap set the scene for a society in which the old virtues of discipline and self-restraint were denigrated' (Edgar, 1986, p. 55). It is not surprising, therefore, that radical right-wing governments have advocated policies designed to restore traditional attitudes pertaining to the family, community life, patriotism and social values.

Radical right traditionalism is revealed in various policy approaches and especially those concerning the family and moral issues. Mrs Thatcher's pronouncements on these subjects are often described as Victorian, but they more accurately connote nineteenth century bourgeois attitudes which extolled heterosexual conjugality, domesticity and wifely subservience to patriarchal authority. Although various thinkers have espoused these values, they have found it difficult to formulate or implement specific policy proposals that will facilitate a return to the idealized norms of Victorian morality. David (1986) reports that a clandestine advisory committee known as the Family Policy Group was appointed by Mrs Thatcher in the early 1980s to develop proposals for the strengthening of the traditional family. But in spite of the involvement of Ferdinand Mount (1982), a respected right-wing family theorist, few concrete recommendations were made. Abbott and Wallace (1989) note that apart from some modifications to the tax system, little has been done to support the traditionalist family ideal through legislative action. Similarly, Gilder's (1982) book which was distributed to the members of the Reagan cabinet, offered few firm proposals for a coherent family policy except to further restrict welfare benefits which, he claimed, had eroded traditional family values. On the other hand, radical right-wing economic policies, coupled with reductions in social expenditures, have had a negative effect on women and children in lower income groups (Abramovitz, 1982).

Attempts to reinforce traditional moral beliefs through legislative action have not been very successful even though activist groups outside government have campaigned vigorously on these issues. In the United States, after Congress rejected the Family Life Protection Bill, campaigns against abortion, pornography, accessible contraception and other sexually related issues intensified. As Bruce (1988) revealed, these campaigns involved highly organized groups of fundamentalist Christians who have made extensive use of civil disobedience tactics to publicize their cause. And, as recent judicial decisions suggest, they have made some headway.

In Britain, where 'moral issues' organizations such as the Festival of Light, the Society for the Unborn Child, and the National Viewers and Listeners Association are not perceived to be particularly powerful, they have nevertheless exerted some influence on government policy. Their major achievement was the enactment of the Video Recordings Act which gave unprecedented power of censorship to the Home Secretary to suppress video material believed to be violent or pornographic. Another indication of the influence of these organizations was the decision by the Director of Public Prosecutions to charge a respected paediatrician with murder for failing to take measures to maintain the life of a severely handicapped infant. Of considerable publicity value for radical right traditionalists was Mrs Gillick's campaign to abrogate government guidelines to physicians for the issuing of contraceptives to teenage women (David, 1986; Abbott and Wallace, 1989).

Patriotism has also featured prominently in the radical right's traditionalist approach. The military excursions of both the British and American governments, and their aggressive posturing on various foreign policy matters have reinforced these ideals. Mrs Thatcher, in particular, opposed several Common Market accords in an effort to assert British autonomy and national pride. Unfortunately, the revival of patriotic fervour has also engendered an increase in racist sentiment, and exploited subterranean populist themes that governments had previously sought to contain.

Discontent, authoritarianism and the appeal of populism

The radical right has made extensive use of populist political strategies in its electoral campaigns. Mrs Thatcher, Mr Reagan and other radical right leaders relied on trusted populist techniques such as the promise of lower taxation, appeals to patriotic sentiment, and the denigration of 'big government' to win electoral support. However, as the history of electoral politics has shown, these techniques are not usually sufficient in themselves to ensure political success. There have been many instances in the past when electorates have voted for tax increases, or supported other issues which have unfavourable immediate consequences. As scholars of populist politics such as Wiles

(1969) and Canovan (1981) have argued, populist electoral strategies are most effective when they exploit popular discontent, and appeal to those sections of the electorate that feel alienated from the political process. And it was the skilful presentation of issues in this way that attracted considerable voter support.

Radical right populist appeal revolved around the two major issues discussed previously in this chapter: firstly, the problems associated with the expansion of statism and secondly, the alleged decline of social order and cherished traditional values. Both were objects of popular discontent at the time. By accentuating these concerns, and offering solutions that were uncomplicated, the radical right demonstrated a congruence with popular sentiment that revealed its own commitment to populist beliefs. At the heart of this ideology is a powerful antipathy to the alienating forces of statism, bureaucracy and government intervention; a belief in self-reliance, individualism, the family and community; a declared commitment to political decentralization and privatization; and a belief that the popular will should find expression in policy making at all levels of government.

In addition to manifesting its own populist ideology, radical right leaders demonstrated an effective ability to use electoral tactics that, in conjunction with their directive leadership style, had considerable effect. In the United States, for example, campaigners like Viguerie, Dolan and New Christian Right organizations such as Moral Majority used mass mailings, telephone banks and the media on an unprecedented scale (Gottfried and Fleming, 1988). Equally important was the way they successfully caricatured and denigrated their political enemies both within and beyond the conservative movement. Radical right strategists were able to create an electoral image of a modernist, left-leaning political establishment that had lost touch with the true ideals and popular will of the masses. This often involved the personal vilification of opponents. In the United States, for example, Dolan and other campaigners adopted smear tactics against liberal politicians as a crude means of bringing them into disrepute. The credentials of the movement's leaders were an added advantage in gaining popular support — Mrs Thatcher extolled her modest origins and effectively juxtaposed them against the aristocratic heritage of the British conservative establishment. Equally important was the successful portrayal of the radical right leadership as decisive, strong and determined. Skilfully manipulating the Iran debacle, Mr Reagan undermined

President Carter's credentials as an effective leader. Mrs Thatcher used similar tactics, encouraging the 'Iron Lady' epithet and luxuriating in her ability to exact loyalty and to discipline her ministers. And it is partly because of the momentum that this approach to statecraft engendered, that both leaders embarked on costly and dubious military ventures abroad.

However, as was suggested earlier, radical right leaders were not simply engaged in a cynical exercise of electoral manipulation. While they revealed a high degree of political acumen, they also demonstrated a congruence between their own beliefs and popular political attitudes. Unlike their predecessors who were struggling to forge intricate solutions to complex problems, they offered commonsensical solutions that were compatible with popular interpretations of contemporary social ills. And in so doing, they appealed to a large, disaffected section of the population that felt neglected by political representatives who had failed to represent their interests.

In its efforts to establish an organic link with popular sentiment, the radical right accentuated the problems of economic stagnation that plagued the 1970s. Although most informed commentators were aware of the disruptive effects of escalating oil prices, capital outflows, and declining industrial investment on the Western economies at the time, the role of these complex causative factors were deliberately neglected in radical right accounts. Instead, the radical right defined contemporary economic problems in terms of a simplistic political economy which, in spite of its academic derivation, was consonant with popular cultural attitudes, particularly in the United States. Central to this analysis was the imputation of negative effects on the economy by statist expansionism, bureaucratic inefficiency, the growth of regulation, the decline of entrepreneurship, excessive taxation, the disruptive tactics of the trade unions, an overly generous welfare system and other factors which, the radical right claimed, were responsible for rapid inflation and stagnant living standards. Its solution had considerable electoral impact because of its homespun flavour and uncomplicated policy prescriptions. The media packaging of this approach in, for example, Mrs Thatcher's ubiquitous analogy between the economy and the household budget, has been enormously successful.

The issue of traditionalism was presented in ways that were equally consonant with popular sentiment. Mrs Thatcher's belief in the central importance of the traditional family is typical of those middle class attitudes which comprise the elemental ingredients of the popular moral order, and which she proudly identifies in her upbringing. Her subscription to other traditionalist themes is equally congruent with popular beliefs. This is revealed most strikingly in her frequent exaltation of patriotism, and highly congruent with the emotive currents that attend issues of nation, culture and race in British society. As Seidel (1986) has shown, similar themes have characterized the populist tendencies of radical right-wing factions in France, the United States and elsewhere.

Race has become a major issue in the generation of popular discontent among a significant section of the electorate. In the United States, the resurgence of racism in recent years can be attributed in part to a backlash against affirmative action and other policy initiatives derived from the civil rights struggle of the 1960s. In Europe, the growth of minority immigrant populations has been viewed with increasing hostility by a proportion of the majority electorate, and this has been exacerbated by the adoption of anti-racist and multicultural programmes by many municipal authorities. As Mitchell and Russell (1989) have shown, programmes such as these have exacerbated the alienation of the white electorate from local politics and they account, to some extent, for the appeal of racist movements, particularly in areas with sizeable minority populations.

The radical right's emphasis on patriotism and nationhood are congruent with the underlying popularity of Social Darwinism in conservative thinking, especially in the United States. It is also congruent with the resurgence of racist sentiments. Mrs Thatcher's public statements on immigration control, and Mr Reagan's opposition to affirmative action have certainly fuelled passions. Ultimately, however, the radical right's populist appeal on issues of race, patriotism and culture lies in its identification of 'the people' with 'the nation' and thus with the white majority electorate. By excluding immigrants, minorities and those of other cultural backgrounds from 'the nation', emotive and organically binding sentiments, which reduce alienation, are generated. These reinforce the movement's populist appeal.

Because of the radical right's emphasis on strong leadership, traditionalism and order, its agenda has not been accompanied by a programme of decentralization and devolution which will enhance the involvement of ordinary people in government, or reduce their alienation from the political process. Instead, most commentators agree that radical right governments have in fact strengthened the central state, placing more emphasis on domestic security, centralized political control and the expansion of military power. The tendency towards political centralization stands in sharp contrast with the movement's programmes for economic liberalization, deregulation and privatization, and is paradoxical in view of its declared intention to give political expression to the popular will. This tendency has been examined by Hall (1983; 1985) who argues that the massive changes involved in breaking the post-war consensus, denationalizing the economy and dismantling of the welfare state require a strong, central government. Since statism has become a way of life, only a powerful authoritarian state can impose a new ideological hegemony on society in which all vestiges of socialist thinking are eradicated. Although Hall's authoritarian populist explanation has been disputed (Jessop *et al.*, 1984; King, 1987), it does seek to address the paradoxes which have characterized radical right-wing policy making over the last decade. It is useful also because it emphasizes the movement's determination to use authoritarianism in its attempt to restructure society and to forge new popular attitudes that are antithetical to collectivism.

Conclusion: the achievements of the radical right

In examining the ideology of the radical right, and reviewing its impact on politics and society, three disparate ideological threads have been identified: these are economic individualism, cultural traditionalism and authoritarian populism. Although these different ideological orientations do not combine readily to form a coherent political platform, the radical right has been able to synthesize these different ideological themes in ways that are easily understood by ordinary people. This is one reason for the movement's electoral success. The paradoxes of combining individualism with cultural traditionalism, and populism with authoritarian statism are not apparent to the movement's supporters who find in its ideological approach, messages they perceive to offer workable solutions to current problems, and hope for a better future. This is not to suggest that non-ideological factors are irrelevant in the success of the radical right. Personal leadership style, statecraft and other factors are also significant. But, by successfully combining these ideological themes, the radical right packaged its message in ways that contrasted with the lack of alternatives offered by its opponents. And, in spite of contradictions in its ideological approach, the movement triumphed in the American and British electoral arenas.

It is questionable, however, whether the radical right can sustain these contradictions. Its attack on the welfare state had populist appeal while it focused on scroungers, cheats, welfare mothers and other folk-devils in popular anti-welfarist mythology, but as social security was threatened in the United States, and the National Health Service in Britain came under attack, the anti-welfarist enterprise has become increasingly risky. Similarly, Mrs Thatcher's cultivated political ruthlessness ceased to have populist impact, and was eventually perceived as an electoral handicap. This factor undoubtedly contributed to her declining parliamentary support and decision to resign. Media image makers have found also that the 'kinder, gentler' sentiments expressed by Mr Bush have electoral resonance, and that the 'greed is good' philosophy of the early 1980s has ceased to be politically attractive.

Few would conclude that the radical right, for all its efforts and successes, has succeeded in breaking the post-war liberal consensus and demolishing the welfare state. Even though the centrist ideologies which sustained the welfare state and legitimized the notion of government intervention in economic and social affairs have been severely shaken, they have survived. The question to be asked then is not whether the welfare state has been destroyed, but to what extent it has been changed, and how it will evolve in the new decade and beyond. This is the question this book seeks to address.

2

The radical right and the welfare state

David Stoesz and James Midgley

The radical right has been extensively concerned with the welfare state. Indeed, the movement's vociferous opposition to the welfare state has been widely reported, and is often identified by journalists and members of the lay public as a primary item on its political agenda. Although other sources of ideological opposition to the welfare state have emerged over the years, none has rivalled the vigour and tenacity of the movement's challenge. And none has so successfully shaken the central tenets of welfarism in the policy arena.

The radical right vigorously opposes state involvement in meeting human needs, advocating instead that the welfare functions presently exercised by government be transferred to individuals, the family, the market, and the voluntary sector. In this respect, the radical right represents a significant departure from established liberal and socialist approaches which differ primarily in the degree to which they advocate state welfare responsibility. The radical right seeks to transcend these approaches by challenging the very notion of state welfare involvement. Radical right thinkers argue that the welfare state is not simply concerned with helping those in need, but is symptomatic of the tendency to institutionalize socialism in the Western industrial nations. The welfare state, they claim, has profound implications for societal organization and human values since it involves the undesirable modification of individualist attitudes, the growth of remote and unaccountable public bureaucracies, the depletion of human and economic resources, the insidious inculcation of collectivist beliefs and the eventual erosion of democratic freedoms. The radical right's attack on the welfare state is thus an integral element of its wider ideological critique of statism.

This chapter will offer a summary of the radical right's position on the welfare state. Focusing the contents of the preceding chapter on issues of social policy, it will show that a variety of arguments are invoked to denigrate the welfare state. It will also seek to examine alternative prescriptions for social welfare offered by radical right social policy makers.

The idea of the welfare state

A central conclusion of most historical studies of social policy is that state responsibility for meeting human needs has increased steadily during the last century (Bruce, 1961; Fraser, 1973; Thane, 1982; Trattner, 1989). In the mid-nineteenth century, state involvement in education, income maintenance, health care and housing was minimal. Governmental involvement in social problems was channelled through the poor laws and, in most countries, its provisions were punitive. State involvement in health care was largely confined to the regulation of sanitary conditions, and the state's role in education was limited to supporting religious and private educational institutions. State housing provision and social work services were non-existent.

By the middle of the twentieth century, however, the situation had changed dramatically. Most industrial countries had introduced comprehensive social security and other income maintenance programmes, and state curative medical care became extensive. State educational services expanded rapidly, and the notion of universal and compulsory education gained worldwide acceptance. In many countries, the state also became extensively involved in the provision of housing; for example, by the 1970s in many European countries, between 25 per cent and 50 per cent of all dwellings were owned and rented to low income families by state housing authorities. State social work services were also introduced and in some countries, such as Britain, most social workers found employment in state agencies. These changes were accompanied by significant increases in state budgetary allocations to the social services. Mishra (1977) estimated that less than 2 per cent of public expenditure was allocated to the social services in Britain in the mid-nineteenth century. By 1980, as Glennerster (1985) revealed, this figure was almost 30 per cent.

In some European countries such as Denmark, the Netherlands and West Germany, social expenditures exceeded a third of public budgets.

Another aspect of the growth of state involvement in welfare has been its ubiquitous character. While the expansion of state welfarism is popularly regarded as a European phenomenon, the trend towards enhanced state welfare provision has occurred throughout the industrial and developing worlds, with nations evidencing varying degrees of social protection. In what is one of the most ambitious attempts to demonstrate empirically the degree of social and economic security afforded through the welfare state, Richard Estes (1984) classified 107 nations according to their level of 'social progress'. Not surprisingly, the most advanced nations, such as Denmark, Sweden, Austria, the Netherlands, New Zealand and Norway scored high on his social progress indicators.

Although the United States is not readily categorized as a welfare state by European, or many American social policy analysts for that matter, the human services have expanded steadily during this century. The American variant of the welfare state has been described as the 'semi-welfare state' (Katz, 1986) and the 'reluctant welfare state' (Jansson, 1988) but, in spite of the incremental nature of its public human service policies, and a widespread cultural antipathy to state welfarism, the European trend towards expanded state involvement in welfare continues to serve as a prototype of welfare provision (Wilensky and Lebeaux, 1965; Karger and Stoesz, 1990).

State involvement in welfare is, of course, a primary characteristic of the communist countries (Madison, 1968; Navarro, 1977; Dixon, 1981; Deacon, 1983) and, as several writers (Hardiman and Midgley, 1982; Midgley, 1984; Jones, 1990) have shown, of many developing countries as well. Although economic realities and other factors have generally precluded governments from making substantial social service budgetary allocations characteristic of European welfare states, the welfarist impulse has not been absent (MacPherson and Midgley, 1987).

The term 'welfare state' has entered the popular vocabulary to connote the extensive involvement of government in the provision, regulation and subsidization of human welfare. The term's provenance is uncertain but British scholars claim that it first came into general use in their country during the mid-1940s, after the publication of the Beveridge Report (Titmuss, 1965; Slack, 1966). However, British scholars have not always been enthusiastic about the term. Marshall noted '"Welfare State" is a term for which I have developed a strong dislike . . .' (Marshall, 1963, p. 245) and Titmuss agreed, pointing out that its use is fraught with real 'dangers' (Titmuss, 1968, p 127). These reservations not only reflect a concern about the concept's imprecision, but about its normative connotations as well.

The normative character of the welfare state idea presents a formidable obstacle to the formulation of a formal, standardized definition. Although many have attempted to use the concept analytically, they have not been able to avoid its normative implications. Accounts of the welfare state seem inevitably to evoke moral and ideological sentiments which draw even the most dispassionate scholars into partisan interpretations. Another problem is that an attempt to define the degree of public sector involvement which is required to classify a country as a welfare state requires some evaluation of the desirability of this involvement. For these and other reasons, no standardized definition of the welfare state has been adopted.

Most formal definitions of the welfare state are explicitly normative. Titmuss's dislike of the term 'welfare state' reflects his belief that it engenders complacency, fostering the erroneous idea that poverty, deprivation and inequality have been eradicated. He was especially critical of writers such as Bell (1960) and Lipset (1960) who had claimed that the institutionalization of the welfare state had finally ended social and ideological cleavages. Titmuss rejected this notion claiming that the welfare state had not met required standards of social justice and egalitarianism. Although he subsequently softened his position, his critique of the concept of the welfare state reflects a normative commitment to a more extensive form of welfarism in which the ideals of altruism, cooperation and community infuse the whole social structure to create what he termed the 'welfare society'. This theme was also developed by other democratic socialist writers such as Myrdal (1960) and Robson (1976).

In this conception, the welfare state (or welfare society) involves a great deal more than the provision of public social services. Although Titmuss and his followers oppose Marxism, their commitment to socialism requires extensive state intervention into both social and economic affairs. This involves the nationalization of the commanding heights of the economy, the extensive regulation of private enterprise, comprehensive economic and social planning through both Keynesian-style demand management and directive planning, the pursuit of full-employment policies, the purposeful redistribution of income, wealth and power, and the provision of a comprehensive and extensive system of state sponsored social services based on universalist rather than selective criteria. The elements of this approach are, of course, similar to Wilensky and Lebeaux's (1965) institutional model of social welfare and, in more recent times, have been developed by Mishra (1984) in his definition of the 'integrated welfare state'. Atherton's (1989) typology also distinguishes between the 'programmatic' welfare state which apportions resources to specific needy populations without explicitly addressing the skewed distribution of wealth, and the 'redistributive' welfare state, which seeks to enhance quality through transferring assets from the wealthy to the poor. It is the redistributive notion of the welfare state, with its emphasis on social justice, to which socialists and left-liberals subscribe.

Definitions which reflect Wilensky and Lebeaux's (1965) residual or Atherton's (1989) 'programmatic' conception of the welfare state have also been popular. Slack quotes one such definition by Peacock who argued that 'the true object of the welfare state is to teach people to do without it' (Slack, 1966, p. 62). Indeed, many definitions of the welfare state have emphasized the notion of minimum standards. Through its many editions, a standard British textbook on the social services taught a generation of students that the distinguishing characteristic of the welfare state was the provision, through government, of the means by which citizens can meet '. . . minimum standards of health, economic security and civilized living' (Hall, 1953, p. 303). Within the American context, Gilbert has located the welfare state within a market economy:

> The welfare state operates through a social market that provides a sort of communal safety net for the casualties of a market economy. Ideally, as a system for distributing benefits in a society, the market economy responds to individual initiative, ability, productivity, and the desire for profit. In contrast, the social market of the welfare state responds to need, dependency, and charitable impulses. (Gilbert, 1983, p. 5)

The residual definition of the welfare state legitimizes the idea of public social service provision but, unlike the institutional approach, does not advocate other forms of state intervention which directly affect productive processes, or seek to alter the distribution of income and wealth. Also, unlike institutionalists, advocates of the residual welfare state are eager advocates of welfare pluralism, closely linking state provisions with voluntary, commercial and other responses. This conception of the welfare state not only limits the role of the state in society, but emphasizes the social service component in state welfarism. Because of the differentiation of the welfare sector from the economic sector, this conception has been described by Mishra (1984) as the 'differentiated welfare state'.

Although located at different ends of the ideological welfare spectrum, both approaches embody a mixed political economy model of society in which governmental social provisions coexist with a liberal polity and market economy. In spite of its advocacy of state regulation of the economy, the redistribution of income and wealth, and the extensive provision of state welfare, the institutional model does not abolish capitalism but seeks instead to reform it. Similarly, the residual welfare state grafts state social services combined with other forms of social provision onto the capitalist economy. It is this element which has been emphasized in more recent publications on the subject. Marshall (1971) is often attributed with having explicated a pluralistic conception of the welfare state in his seminal account of 'welfare capitalism' but he attributes this notion to the British politician, Richard Crossman. Robson (1976) reports that the term had earlier been used by the Dutch author Thoenes (1966) to differentiate the welfare state from the liberal free-market state which preceded it, and the contemporary communist state with which it was competing.

Coupled with the notion of welfare capitalism is the idea of welfare pluralism which, developing the residualist conception of the welfare state, advocates the institutionalization of a variety of formal responses to human need. The state is not regarded as the only or even primary provider of welfare services, but is seen as one of several partners in a complex welfare mix of private, voluntary and other forms of social provision. According to Kamerman (1983), the 'mixed welfare economy' includes not-for-profit agencies, governmental social programmes, and the market. In his 'theory of social assignments', Walzer (1986) proposes four entities that are central to understanding welfare: the family, the market, the state, and the social sector. With a slight change in wording, these groups are identical to those proposed by Johnson (1987). Stoesz (1988a) presented a 'structural interest' approach, identifying four sectors of the welfare state: the voluntary sector, the governmental sector, the corporate sector, and private practice.

The idea of welfare pluralism and the mixed welfare economy stands in contradistinction to Titmuss's commitment to institutionalism, but it has gained favour among many advocates of state welfarism. Among them are some of Titmuss's former students such as Pinker (1979) who has developed the normative elements in this idea extensively. Criticizing Titmuss for juxtaposing the residual–institutional typology in a way that ensures the moral superiority of the institutionalist position, Pinker argues that the mixed economy approach represents a third and highly desirable model of welfare which is not 'consistent with either capitalism or socialism'. He argues further that 'its influence has already been sufficiently pervasive to create a new social system which will subsequently develop without regard for either of these doctrines' (Pinker, 1979, p. 243). In this 'mercantile collectivist' approach to welfare, the dangers of extreme collectivism and individualism are avoided. The socialist tendency towards totalitarianism is effectively obviated by the institutionalization of liberal democracy while the callous neglect of human need under conditions of extreme individualism is prevented through the institutionalization of welfarism.

It is perhaps ironic that at the time Pinker (1979) was writing, two doctrinaire schools of individualist and collectivist thought were gaining ascendancy in social policy circles to challenge the very concept of the welfare state. Transcending the previous debate, both the radical right and the increasingly influential Marxian or 'radical' school of social policy attacked the welfare state. Left-radicals defined the welfare state not as a beneficial societal formation, but as functional to the needs of capitalism, and suppressive of the true aspirations of the working class (Cloward and Piven, 1971; Gough, 1979; Ginsburg, 1979; Offe, 1984). They implied that since the welfare state operates as an instrument of capitalism, its abolition through revolutionary action is to be welcomed. Paradoxically, the Marxian left's rejection of the welfare state was congruent with the radical right's critique although, after the movement's ascendancy, Marxists joined in condemning the radical right's anti-welfarist onslaught. In so doing, they justified the continuation of the welfare state on the ground that it offers an arena within which the working class can confront the forces of capital and effect significant social changes (Piven and Cloward, 1982).

Before the radical right emerged as an effective political force, writers such as Seldon (1960), Lees (1961) and Harris and Seldon (1965; 1979) at the Institute of Economic Affairs in London had waged a lonely war against state welfarism, regarding Titmuss's institutionalist ideas as pure anathema. Even the residual 'differentiated' welfare state, they argued, was unacceptable. Instead, they advocated the abolition of the welfare state and the transfer of its functions to the market, the voluntary sector and the family. Evoking images of the Victorian poor law, they reluctantly accepted that minimal state support for a safety net, administered by the voluntary or commercial sectors, should cater for those in desperate need. With the election of Mrs Thatcher in Britain and Mr Reagan in the United States, these ideas were receptively examined by policy makers.

The radical right critique of the welfare state

The central ingredients of the radical right's case against the welfare state are concerned with issues of responsibility, efficiency, freedom, and prosperity. The movement contends that the welfare state is a governmental institution managed by a liberal or socialist elite which has weakened traditional values of hard work, responsibility and sobriety, created a large and inefficient bureaucratic state welfare apparatus, intruded excessively into the private lines of citizens diminishing choice and individual preferences, and harmed economic productivity and growth.

The radical right's critique of the welfare state is decidedly populist and sectarian. Government welfare programmes are faulted for a breakdown in mutual obligations between groups, a lack of attention to efficiencies in the way programmes are operated and benefits awarded, the induced dependency of beneficiaries on programmes, and the growth of the welfare industry and its special interest groups, particularly professional associations. Radical right thinkers believe that the welfare state erodes individual responsiblity and initiative. By fostering 'dependence' on welfare, beneficiaries of the social services need not work hard, save, or act in a responsible manner. Rather than alleviate destitution, welfare state programmes induce dependency and the proliferation of a culture of poverty. The New Right solution, then, is to replace dysfunctional (liberal) values with functional (conservative) values: 'delayed gratification, work and saving, commitment to family and to the next generation, education and training, self-improvement, and rejection of crime, drugs, and casual sex' (Institute for Cultural Conservatism, 1987, p. 83).

The most recent manifestation of the culture of poverty notion is the contention that an 'underclass' has emerged in nations with welfare states. While most underclass sightings have occurred in the United States (Glasgow, 1981; Auletta, 1982; Lemann, 1986; Wilson, 1987), other commentators have made similar observations in Britain (Murray, 1990) and Japan (Schoenberger, 1990). According to the radical right, the underclass is a direct product of the unconditional social programmes offered by the welfare state which do not obligate beneficiaries to behave conventionally in order to receive benefits.

The radical right also alleges that the welfare state is economically detrimental to a market economy. According to the tenets of supply-side economic theory, to which many of the radical right subscribe, government expenditures must be reduced since they are derived from taxes, monies that the private sector needs for capitalization. Supply-side theorists hold that government competes with the private sector by levying taxes on private revenue, in effect starving the goose that lays the golden egg. This economic position appeals to the radical right, since a major consequence is substantial tax cuts. The movement has been able to use supply-side economics to offer middle and working class people substantial reductions in their tax obligations. Furthermore, reductions in corporate taxes favour small business, so the radical right is able to appeal to that constituency as well.

Radical right advocates also argue that the relatively high tax rates of advanced welfare states also reduce profit margins and thus impede entrepreneurial incentives to invest and produce. Eventually, the demand of welfare recipients for more benefits outstrips the capacity of a market economy to provide these benefits without losing its competitive edge. As a *Time* report claimed:

> At its present levels, the welfare apparatus has simply become too expensive for most governments, and their taxpayers. Across Europe, social security systems are grappling with fiscal crisis, in part because ponderous, costly bureaucracies have mushroomed to administer a vast array of programs that sometimes neglect the essential to serve up what is merely desirable. Bloated beyond its architects' intent, welfarism is threatening bankruptcy in some countries. (Painton and Malkin, 1981, p. 32)

As successive governments have tried to expand the welfare state even further to meet people's aspirations, government 'overload' has become increasingly evident.

The radical right also contends that the welfare state is symptomatic of the increasing intrusion of the state into private life, and that it is a harbinger of totalitarianism. The authoritarian aspects of the welfare state have several features. Fiscally, the welfare state functions from involuntary contributions (taxes) which individuals are compelled to pay. This is repugnant since all citizens must, therefore, pay for services they do not need, and which they may even find morally disagreeable. Administratively, the welfare state enjoys a monopoly of benefit provision. Except in those instances where government contracts out services, beneficiaries of welfare state services do not enjoy the same choice of providers as do others purchasing services in the market. As a result, beneficiaries may be 'locked in' to benefits that are not as good or adequate as those available to other citizens. A particularly objectionable aspect of the welfare state to the radical right is the professional associations which operate social programmes. Because social welfare professionals are authorized to protect the vulnerable from the predations of others, social workers are free to violate the privacy of the family to intervene on behalf of abused and neglected children and elders. Thus, 'the rampant interventionism of the state' occurs at the expense of 'autonomy of the family' (Berger and Berger, 1983, p. 210).

As a related point, the radical right contends that the true purpose of the welfare state is to further the interests of its constituent groups. A cadre of human service professionals such as health care personnel, social workers, psychologists, counsellors and administrators would be out of work if the welfare state was abolished. The expansion of the welfare state actually benefits the professionals who are employed by the government or who are dependent on government contracts. This argument received credence when James Buchanan received the Nobel Prize in economics. According to Buchanan's 'public choice theory', government is unable to resist demands for increased expenditures through social programmes because the mobilization of advocacy groups is carefully targeted at decision-makers, yet costs are spread widely throughout the population through taxes. As programmes expand, governmental deficits are unavoidable. Adherents to public choice theory view social welfare as a series of concessions to disadvantaged groups that could be endless, eventually bankrupting government (Karger and Stoesz, 1990, p. 15).

According to the radical right, the welfare state continues to operate, despite its dysfunctional features, because it is controlled by an élite which is out of touch with the populace. This view is particularly widespread in the United States. This élite which is comprised of professionals who are educated at exclusive universities and who adhere to secular and liberal values, has created a 'new class' which endeavours to institute policies which are contrary to those preferred by ordinary people. A primary vehicle of the liberal élite is the welfare state, which it controls through sympathetic politicians and self-interested professionals. Liberal politicians legislate programmes and liberal professionals administer them, all quite independent of public influence, although the public pays through taxes. Instrumental in the activities of the liberal élite are private policy institutes, the liberal think-tanks, which are bankrolled by wealthy liberals and professional organizations to provide the grist for the self-serving programmes of the welfare state (Stoesz, 1981; Judis, 1990b).

This objection, which the radical right has made accessible to the uninformed public through its electoral campaigns, is now a coherent critique: a liberal, secular élite promulgates legislation which advances their own interests through welfare programmes. The dysfunctional nature of welfare programmes produces additional social problems for which there are additional calls for more welfare programmes. Thus, the welfare state assures the continued expansion of benefits. All of this is at public expense and the costs escalate to the point that government runs into serious deficit. Ultimately, citizens revolt as their taxes exceed the social benefits they perceive to be coming from the welfare state.

Welfare and the radical right

The overarching strategy of the radical right toward the welfare state is to replace government with other social institutions including the informal sector, the family, the non-profit voluntary sector, and the proprietary commercial sector, as a basis of welfare provision. This has been clearly articulated by radical right-wing ideologues in the United States who have advocated 'shifting more responsibility from the federal government to state and local governments and private institutions' (Anderson, 1980, p. 104). Radical right opposition to the welfare state received a measure of academic respectability when Berger and Neuhaus (1977) advanced their influential theory of 'mediating structures' as researchers at the American Enterprise

Institute, a Washington DC think-tank. According to their formulation, the fundamental problem confronting modern culture is the growth of 'megastructures' (big government, big business, big professions and big labour), and a corresponding diminution of the individual. The route to empowering people is to revitalize mediating structures such as the neighbourhood, family, church, and voluntary association. In a subsequent analysis, Novak, another scholar at the American Enterprise Institute, argued that the business corporation was not in fact, as Berger and Neuhaus had claimed, a 'megastructure' but rather a mediating structure capable of linking ordinary people together and enhancing their identification with the social order. In this way, Novak effectively cast government, labour and the professions (the basic institutions of the liberal social reform movement) as the source of mass alienation (Novak, 1981). From this orientation, radical right-wing tactics regarding the welfare state are fairly straightforward arguing for the containment, if not reversal of governmental social programmes, while enhancing the welfare capacity of other social institutions.

Three such alternative welfare institutions may be readily identified in radical right social policy proposals: they are the family, the voluntary sector and the commercial sector. In addition, while the movement denigrates the state as a provider of social welfare, the utilization of the state for purposes of changing social attitudes and modifying social institutions is readily advocated.

Welfare and the family

For the radical right, welfare should be a normal function of family life and ideally there would be no need for public welfare provision at all. Yet, the radical right senses acutely that the family is besieged by a multitude of hostile forces which are inimical to it performing its traditional welfare role: homosexuals and female liberationists threaten the traditional social relations between the sexes; the state subverts family financial independence through extortionate taxation; and human service professionals, usually in collusion with the state, intrude into the privacy of the home. The political expression of these sensitivities strikes directly at the welfare state since the social services often support women outside of the strictures of traditional, patriarchal family life. Taxation for welfare programmes not only robs families of income that they increasingly need to make ends meet, but also goes toward providing services, such as abortion and income support for female-headed households, which the radical right contends are ruinous to family life. Finally, government sanctioned human service workers continually violate the right to privacy of the family usually under the guise of protecting the rights of children (Berger and Berger, 1983).

The radical right believes that the family's traditional welfare functions can only be revitalized if the family itself is revitalized as the basic institution in Western society. In the United States, support for the beleaguered family has been summed up by the Institute for Cultural Conservatism (1987) whose prescriptions for strengthening family life have been echoed elsewhere. The organization argues firstly that the traditional nuclear family must be restored. This requires that one parent, the mother, remain in the home permanently to raise children. The family can only fulfil its traditional welfare function if the vast majority of American children are nurtured in this type of environment. It is necessary, secondly, to reduce the incidence of divorce, out-of-wedlock pregnancy, abortion, and pre-marital sex. As was shown in the previous chapter of this book, the decline in moral standards has been identified as a major cause of social decline in the industrial nations by radical right-wing thinkers. Thirdly, the values on which stable families depend, including responsibilities to and for offspring, disapproval of extra-marital sex, and reverence for life, both before and after birth, must be promoted. Next, the legal standing of the family, including a presumption of the reasonableness of parental action, must be recognized. Legislative, administrative and judicial actions which work to undermine the traditional family, must be voided. The economic well-being of the family must also be restored. This can be achieved by making it possible for single wage-earner families to maintain a middle-class standard of living. Finally, governmental indifference toward the traditional family must be replaced with government recognition and support for its vital functional roles.

In the event that the immediate, nuclear family is unable to be self-sufficient, members of the extended family, friends and neighbours are preferred sources of assistance. Often such support is 'informal', the classic example being the American custom of community barn raising. Such activities reinforce existing social ties and they make assistance a highly personal affair. While the needy are immediately known to neighbours and support is offered prudently, there is little rationale for providing aid to the non-conformist or one who is foreign, the 'stranger'.

The importance of the voluntary sector

To the extent that welfare is beyond the means of the family and the informal sector, the radical right prefers that assistance be provided through the organized voluntary sector. The voluntary sector embodies virtues that are dear to traditionalists such as neighbourliness, self-reliance and community solidarity. Not surprisingly, a special place is reserved for the Church in the radical right's social policy. Many of the non-profit agencies of the voluntary sector are sectarian and are directly controlled by religious institutions. Moreover, since any altruistically-minded group may obtain the tax-exempt status so essential for voluntary sector operations, many groups associated with the radical right have established their own social agencies, sometimes in direct opposition to established voluntary sector agencies. A good example is Birthright, an American anti-abortion organization that encourages birth and adoption, counter to Planned Parenthood, a liberal organization which provides abortion among other reproductive health services.

In the United States, there is ample precedent for the substitution of governmental programmes by the voluntary sector. For the past two decades, the federal government has allowed states to subcontract with voluntary agencies for the provision of social services funded through the Title XX Social Services Block Grant legislation. By the late 1980s, 42 per cent of the $2.7 billion allocated by the federal government for social services went to 'private/voluntary providers under purchase of service agreements' (United States, 1990, p. 748). Most established voluntary sector agencies are affiliated with the United Way which collects funds for member agencies, many of which also count on governmental contracts. Sectarian agencies, such as the Salvation Army, Catholic Charities, Lutheran Social Services and Episcopal Community Services are free to match their social service policies and programmes to the religious values espoused by their respective denominations. In so doing, sectarian agencies function much as 'mediating structures', providing a personalizing element to the depersonalization which right-wing critics claim is characteristic of the welfare state bureaucracy. Undoubtedly, if there is to be dependency among the destitute, the radical right would prefer that it be on voluntary sector agencies, rather than under the auspice of welfare state. Most recently, the visibility of the voluntary sector has been highlighted by President Bush's appeal to 'a thousand points of light'; the notion that the nation's social problems can best be addressed by the voluntary impulses of citizens.

Welfare for profit in the commercial sector

Within democratic-capitalist welfare states, the commercialization of human services has proceeded rapidly during the last two decades. Proprietary firms have exploited markets in nursing care, hospital management, health maintenance organizations, child day care, and even corrections (Stoesz, 1986). While the majority of human service corporations are secular in orientation, most religious denominations have special subsidiaries for the purpose of developing retirement communities for retirees and the chronically ill. Significantly, much proprietary human service activity in the United States has appeared in the South and West, areas which are also hot-beds of radical right ideology. However, the relationship between a competitive corporate sector and the radical right is not always consonant, primarily because commercial pressures frequently disrespect or subvert traditional values promoted by the movement. An important attempt to reconcile such differences is Michael Novak's *Toward a Theology of the Corporation* (1981) in which he rationalized theological opposition to the state and extolled the virtues of the commercial sector:

> I advise intelligent, ambitious, and morally serious young Christians and Jews to awaken to the growing dangers of statism. They will better save their souls and serve the cause of the Kingdom of God all around the world by restoring the liberty and power of the private sector than by working for the state. I propose for the consideration of theologians the notion that the prevailing moral threat in our era may not be the power of the corporations but the growing power and irresponsibility of the state. (Novak, 1981, p. 28)

As Novak suggests, radical right-wing advocates regard the corporate sector as a preferred vehicle of service delivery over the state. As an instrument of the market, the corporation is a manifestation of free enterprise, and thus consistent with American traditionalism. Such ideas also find support among the fundamentalist New Christian Right which, in spite of holding strong traditional values, believes in the sanctity of the profit motive. As Midgley (1990) revealed in a recent account of the New Christian Right's attitude towards the welfare state, the replacement of government social services with commercial provision is readily endorsed on the ground that this is consonant with religious belief; as he noted, fundamentalist Christians believe that 'individualist values, hard work, and the acquisition of property and wealth is divinely inspired' (Midgley, 1990, p. 97).

In spite of the movement's suspicions of the established professions, private practice is also compatible with the radical right's enthusiastic endorsement of human service corporations. Since private human service professionals are independent businesspersons, they demonstrate the values of productivity, private property and autonomy so dearly held by the radical right. It is the congruence of these ideas with the basic tenets of American culture that have long protected the medical profession from attempts to 'socialize' medical care in that country. Private practice also appeals to conservatively-inclined professionals who object to practising in agencies maintained by the welfare state. In this regard, an organization of Christian social workers has been established in the United States. Although most traditionalists would prefer that social problems be managed within the private domain of the family; but, in instances when that is not possible, a like-minded professional may be acceptable. In order to establish lucrative practices, however, independent social workers who are sympathetic to the radical right would have to be perceived by clients as having shed their liberal, secular tendencies.

Using the state

Despite rhetorical antipathy toward government, the radical right has demonstrated increasing sophistication in using the state to advance its objectives. In the United States, the radical *New Right* faction of the Republican Party engaged in feverish electoral activities in the late 1970s to ensure the election of Mr Reagan in the hope that he would use the considerable amount of state power at his disposal to terminate the welfare state. In Chile, General Pinochet effectively used the coercive power of his military machine in an attempt to foster new attitudes and institutions. Another example of this tendency was the mobilization of fundamentalist Christian conservatives for political purposes by evangelical organizations such as Moral Majority, and the 1988 bid of 'televangelist' preacher, Pat Robertson, for the presidency. Although Mr Robertson did poorly in the primaries, he has not been daunted and has now founded an organization called the Christian Coalition which seeks 'to train conservative Christians to shape government policy'. Drawing on his 1.8 million member presidential campaign mailing list, Robertson expects to have 150,000 members in 500 local chapters by 1991 (Chandler, 1990, p. A5). As a sequel to the now-defunct Moral Majority, the Christian Coalition represents a major new effort to routinize New Christian Right aspirations in politics.

The radical right has used the policy instruments of the state in an attempt to weaken the welfare state. Because of considerable political opposition to their agenda, this has been a gradual and insidious process rather than a direct frontal abolitionist endeavour. The movement's public policy objectives have proceeded along several fronts. First, it has attempted to contain the expansion of governmental social services. Because social insurance programmes do reflect the traditionalist concern for work, these have been spared, but means-tested programmes have not been so fortunate. Services for the poor have borne the brunt of radical right-wing wrath directed at those alleged to be dependent, slothful and illicit. In the United States, with the support of mainstream conservatives, the radical right has been successful at containing the expansion of poverty programmes. The radical right also advocates the replacement of welfare policy with tax policy. In the United States, this has meant an increasing reliance on the Earned Income Tax Credit (EITC) operated by the Treasury Department. Hence, during the 1980s the EITC expanded while income maintenance programmes under the auspice of the Department of Health and Human Services were held in check. The radical right has used public policy to impose its values on other citizens. The denial of federal funds for the purposes of aiding poor women in obtaining abortions in the United States is the clearest example of this. Politicians were instrumental in the incorporation of tough 'workfare' requirements in the Family Support Act of 1988, a conservative welfare reform initiative which demanded that welfare beneficiaries engage in job-related activities as a condition for receipt of benefits (Karger and Stoesz, 1990).

In its effort to use the power of government to weaken the welfare state, the radical right has also advanced market-oriented strategies in service provision, such as vouchers, as a method for breaking up the welfare state 'monopoly' in areas such as health and education. The preoccupation with constitutional amendments which would abridge extant reproductive rights as well as the separation of church and state further illustrates attempts to use public policy to impose traditional values on others. Thus, the radical right has not been negligent of the use of government policy to advance its ends. There have been similar developments in Britain where budgetary reductions, the advocacy of vouchers and so-called 'internal markets' within state social service programmes and other devices have all been used deliberately as instruments of public policy to damage the welfare state.

The radical right and the future of the welfare state

International dynamics, particularly the rapid development of the global economy, have contributed to the radical right becoming a transnational phenomenon. The proliferation of the 'stateless corporation' has broken down the integrity of national political jurisdictions, effectively subverting the capacity of national governments to control vital features of their internal economies. As a result, a multitude of developing Third World economies are pitted against those of capitalist nations. Deterioration of living standards in the advanced industrial economies contributes to the popularity of the radical right. Furthermore, the demise of state-driven political economies of the communist, second world has boosted the cause of right-wing theorists. Taking an international view of national development, for example, Milton and Rose Friedman (1988) have posited three 'tides' of political-economic events which they argue have swept over entire nations: the rise of *laissez-faire* (the Adam Smith tide), the rise of the welfare state (the Fabian tide), and the resurgence of free markets (the Hayekian tide). To the extent that conservative governments control the capitalist nation-states, while the state-dominated communist economies disintegrate, pro-governmental orientations to the welfare state will be challenged.

Given these international developments, the radical right can make a credible case that it is on the right side of history in its effort to engineer social affairs. Its critique of the liberal welfare consensus has been carefully formulated. Its agenda is also clear. Gaining political power in different countries during the 1980s, the movement had the ideological commitment, theoretical orientation and political opportunity to put its anti-welfarist beliefs into practice. The remaining chapters of this book will seek to assess to what extent its agenda has been implemented in different societies in different parts of the world.

Part II

Implementation and experiences

3

The radical right and the welfare state in Britain: pensions and health care

Howard Glennerster

A common view one meets in America, Europe and other parts of the world is that the modern welfare state was founded in Britain, that it had, until the economic crisis of the mid-1970s, one of the most generous levels of welfare anywhere in the world and that Mrs Thatcher's decade in power has largely destroyed or privatized that legacy. Some more academic observers have drawn encouragement from a similar set of observations — having led the world into the welfare mess the British are now showing the world the way out (Olsen, 1989). Other authors from the opposite political perspective see social policy in Britain as the invention of a narrow intellectual élite that never had a well-grounded theoretical or class base and simply collapsed when faced with a tough ideological alternative (Mishra, 1984). None of these simplistic views stand up to examination in the light of a decade of conservative government.

The British welfare state

Britain was not the originator of most of the elements of a modern welfare state. Social insurance was copied from Bismarkian Prussia, free education came later than in any other advanced nation, nor was expenditure on these services conspicuously generous by international standards in the 1970s (see Table 3.1). Only in the case of the National Health Service did Britain have an innovation that was startlingly bold, or foolhardy, according to taste. Introduced in 1948, it had

Table 3.1 Social expenditures* in OECD countries as percentages of GDP (1960 and 1981)

	1960	1981
Denmark	n.a.	33.3
West Germany	20.5	31.5
Austria	17.9	27.7
Belgium	17.4	37.6
Italy	16.8	29.1
Netherlands	16.2	36.1
Sweden	15.4	33.4
Finland	15.4	25.9
United Kingdom	13.9	23.7
France	13.4	29.5
New Zealand	13.0	19.6
Canada	12.1	21.5
Ireland	11.7	28.4
Norway	11.7	27.1
United States	10.9	20.8
Australia	10.2	18.8
Greece	8.5	13.4
Japan	8.0	17.5
Switzerland	7.7	14.9
OECD average (unweighted)	13.1	25.6

*Direct public expenditure on education, health, pensions, unemployment and other income maintenance. Housing is excluded.

Source: OECD (1985). See also Hills (1990).

given every citizen the right to free and comprehensive health care at the point of use, paid for out of central government taxation. In the subsequent decades the principle of completely free access had been eroded and small charges were levied on drugs and higher ones on dentures and optician's services and spectacles, but access to the local doctor and hospital remained free.

What was unusual about Britain was the comprehensive nature of its welfare provisions, especially for those outside the normal social insurance net, the compressed and significant timescale during which the major modern elements were put in place and the coherent philosophical base which underlay the provisions.

State involvement in public health, education, housing, pensions, unemployment and sickness had grown steadily throughout the nineteenth century and on to the 1930s (Thane, 1982; Thompson, 1990), but the interventions were *ad hoc* and selective, targeted on the poorer sections of the population. What the legislation of 1944–8 did was to introduce a set of comprehensive national services which developed in coverage during the next thirty years. The benefit levels were never generous. Hampered by Britain's slow rate of economic growth they fell increasingly behind average levels in Europe and made more use of means testing. However, the national system of public assistance that underpinned the social insurance benefits did provide a safety net for the very poorest more effective than the more expensive systems in most of continental Europe (Walker, Lawson and Townsend, 1984).

The theoretical underpinning of these institutions reached into the popular consciousness. There was a rich legacy of political ideas in the early part of the twentieth century that accumulated into a powerful case for state intervention and the rights of individual citizens (Barker, 1978). The Beveridge Report (1942) was unusually wide-ranging and explicit in its values. Though Winston Churchill and the Treasury were cool about its utopian goals it came to be used by the war-time propaganda machine to encapsulate a vision of a free post-war Britain and was expounded to British servicemen and servicewomen as well as the home population. The coterminous impact of Keynesian economic theory is difficult to exaggerate. Marshall (1950) and later Titmuss (1958) forged a set of ideas that gave both a feeling of inevitability and moral certainty to these post-war developments. Nothing comparable is to be found in other countries' literature.

Marshall argued that the legislation we have referred to was the culmination of Britons' long march to full citizenship. They had first won from their monarchs the basic legal rights to freedom from arbitrary arrest, freedom of speech and freedom of worship. Using Berlin's (1969) later formulation we can see these as establishing a citizen's negative freedoms, his or her right *not* to be interfered with by arbitrary state power. Next came Britons' right to political freedom, full adult suffrage, gained only relatively a short time before this. Finally came the positive freedoms — the right 'to be and to do' as Amartya Sen (1990) has put it recently, or as Beveridge put it at the time: 'freedom from Want, Disease, Ignorance, Squalor and Idleness'. These negative and positive freedoms were, and this was the central point, interdependent. One was useless without the others. Here was a powerful political basis for the welfare state. It was this that the *New Right* came to challenge, by shifting attention back to the overwhelming importance of negative and political freedom as it saw it.

Thus, the impact of the radical right on social policy in Britain is of particular interest and significance because if traditional welfare values were to be entrenched anywhere, this was the place. Moreover, the political and economic system in Britain gave the radical right its best chance outside Chile. Britain's economy had been declining relative to other industrialized countries since the 1870s. By the time of the oil crisis of the mid-1970s the average income per head had fallen behind all but the agricultural Mediterranean states of Western Europe. High inflation and the perception that the trade unions were to blame, gave the Conservative government a wide popular brief to attack the labour movement and all that it stood for. Once elected, the powers of the Conservative government were all powerful, especially since it was unrestrained by any effective opposition. The Labour party's own defence policy and internal battles together destroyed its electoral appeal. Mrs Thatcher led the *New Right* faction in the Tory party and had almost total unrivalled power for more than a decade. Surely, if the radical right was to come into its kingdom, the United Kingdom was the place to do it.

The impact of the radical right

Goodbye to full employment

It will be recalled from Chapter 1 that there are several strands to the radical right movement and they are well illustrated in the sequence of events in Britain. The need to contain what threatened to be rampant inflation (over 25 per cent) in the wake of the oil shock led to the first defeat for the old order. The Labour government in 1976 accepted the medicine prescribed by the International Monetary Fund (IMF), albeit reluctantly. This led to the explicit abandonment of Keynesian budgetary policy, the adoption of monetary targets and cuts in public spending after 1976, three years before Mrs Thatcher came to office (Glennerster, 1977). Like many other less well developed nations, Britain was at the mercy of economic forces beyond its control. The rise in unemployment that followed the Labour government's deflation was moderate compared to what was to follow. The government adopted a deliberately 'corporatist' approach, seeking trade union support for dampening wage demands. Nor did the Labour government abandon any of its social programmes, it merely cut expenditure on them. Even so the break with the past was decisive and the new set of social and economic priorities that were to last for the next fifteen years began at that time.

Unlike President Reagan who accepted the comfortable Laffer doctrine that reduced tax rates would generate more revenue in the short as well as the long run (Stockman, 1985), Mrs Thatcher remained a true disciple of Milton Friedman and financed her early income tax cuts by sharp increases in indirect taxation, nearly doubling value added tax, and increasing social security tax. Even by the end of the 1980s this left the average household paying a higher share of its income in tax than when Mrs Thatcher's government came to power. By 1989 there was a large budget surplus. In the early years of the new Conservative administration, high interest rates, a higher sterling exchange rate and reduced public spending on capital expenditure especially, produced the sharpest recession Britain had experienced since the 1930s. It was this part of the radical right's programme that dominated the Conservative government's agenda for its first term. Despite the unpopularity of unemployment subsequent elections and public opinion polls showed that for most of the electorate inflation was the prime concern and, if high unemployment was necessary to defeat it, it was a price the employed were prepared to see the unemployed pay. The abandonment of full employment policy, and the public's acceptance of it, was the most unambiguous victory for the radical right. The importance of traditional social policy in making that economic restructuring possible will be returned to later in this chapter.

Expenditure restraint

The second major objective of this early period was to cut back on public expenditure. Despite increasingly tough measures to cut local authorities' expenditure on education, housing and personal social services, the paradox was that by more than trebling the level of unemployment in less than two years the cost of unemployment benefit pushed up the total spent on social policy. The result was that in the first years of Mrs Thatcher's first term the share of the GDP going into social security expenditure actually rose sharply. The pursuit of macroeconomic objectives counteracted the success of the narrower public spending goals. Overall, what both governments succeeded in doing after 1976 was not to cut the scale of state activity but to

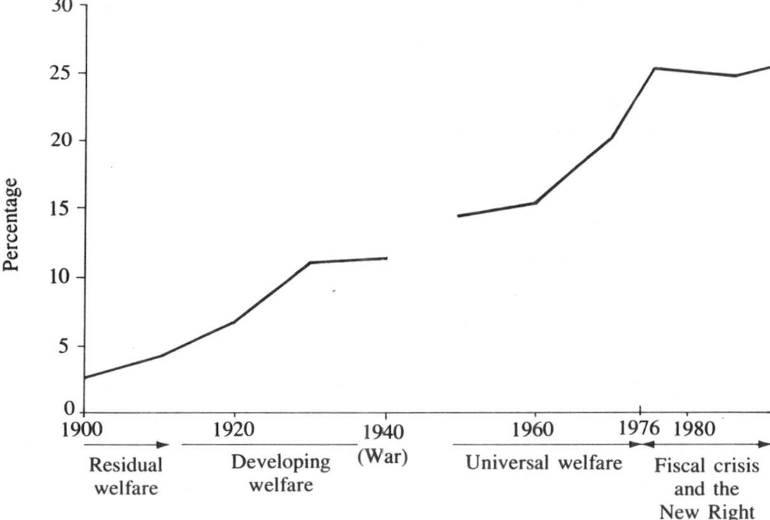

Figure 3.1 Social spending and the UK economy: the cost of social services as a percentage of GDP (*Sources:* Peacock and Wiseman, 1961; and CSO *National Income and Expenditure* for relevant years)

stabilize the share of the national income spent by government on social welfare (see Figure 3.1). We are defining social welfare here as national and local public expenditure on education, health, social care, housing and social security. The share of total public spending going to social welfare, about half, also remained unchanged through the period 1976 to 1990. The essential change which the 1980s brought was an end to the growing scale of social spending. The impact of this sharp change in the long-term growth pattern should not be minimized, but at the same time it is important to be clear what Mrs Thatcher succeeded in doing. This was to check the growing share of resources being devoted to social expenditure, not to reduce them.

Within the overall total, however, there have been significant changes in the shares taken by the different services. Only the social care and social work services retained their slice of the social cake, at 3–4 per cent of all social spending. Expenditure on the National Health Service increased its share from 18 per cent to 21 per cent, social security increased its share from 35 per cent to 45 per cent, while education fell from 25 per cent to 20 per cent and direct spending on public housing fell most from 17 per cent to 8 per cent, though part of this decline was the result of a shift from a general housing subsidy to a means-tested social security based system. Total welfare expenditure on transfers, or cash benefits, rose by two-thirds in real terms over the period 1974–88 and other current expenditure rose by half in real terms. Capital expenditure fared worst, down from 15 per cent of all social spending to 5 per cent. A detailed account of the trends for each service in the United Kingdom and an assessment of their impact on service outcomes can be found in a London School of Economics study, *The State of Welfare* (Hills, 1990).

A new set of influences

From the late 1940s onwards the Conservative party had come to accept the broad structure of the post-war welfare state and, indeed, had extended it in important respects. It had competed with the Labour party in the late 1950s and 1960s to improve services and extend educational opportunity. The extent of agreement should not be exaggerated, but the Conservative party had never proposed major structural change that would have dismantled any part of the system. There had been two abortive attempts to extend the scope of the private sector, one in rented housing in the mid-1950s, and the other in pensions in the 1970s but neither succeeded. Throughout the 1960s one group of liberal economists had ploughed a lone furrow, essentially interpreting Milton Friedman's ideas to a British audience. They produced pamphlets under the imprint of the Institute for Economic Affairs (IEA). They argued for a free market in health care, for vouchers and student loans in education to replace free higher education and student support. They had argued against public housing and for a free market in private landlord property and for income-tested benefits. After Mrs Thatcher became leader of the Conservative party these ideas began to be taken seriously. The IEA was joined by other think-tanks — the Centre for Policy Studies was founded shortly after Mrs Thatcher became leader by her close associates to provide a new style of policy advice. The Adam Smith Institute was added later, and other groups followed. These were linked into Mrs Thatcher's own policy staff at 10 Downing Street and were used to generate ideas for new policies untainted by the traditional Civil Service in the social departments. Following the public choice theorists' conclusions, it was assumed that civil servants would be incapable of producing plans for their own demise.

It took time for these ideas to reach the social policy agenda. Apart from the harsh expenditure constraints imposed in Mrs Thatcher's first term, virtually no significant changes were attempted in the social field. The massive selling off of the public sector industries, the removal of various trade union rights, the increasingly severe penalties imposed on local authorities that spent more than the government's norms, all this was quite enough for the government to handle. One policy was both structural and popular — giving public housing tenants the right to buy their own property at a bargain price. This reduced the share of all housing owned by the state from 33 per cent to 26 per cent within a decade. At that point the policy stuck because despite the knock-down prices the remaining tenants were unwilling or unable to buy. Another more limited policy innovation from this early period is interesting because it appears to be the only remaining vestige of the Friedmanite idea of educational vouchers — 35,000 pupils from lower income families were able to take places at private schools paid for by the national exchequer. In fact, this was merely the reintroduction of a similar scheme that had existed since 1902 which had been wound up by the previous Labour government in 1976.

It was not until Mrs Thatcher's second term that any attempt was made at structural reform to a mainstream service and that was aimed at the largest component of social spending — social security.

Structural changes attempted

There were two main grounds for choosing to tackle social security first. Constituting half of all social spending, it was also the fastest growing element. Unemployment and more generous pension levels promised by the previous Labour government to a growing aged population, were the most important reasons for present and future growth. If this could be checked it would go a long way to meeting the government's primary aim of reducing public expenditure. The other reason for tackling social security first was closely linked to the government's broader economic strategy. Radical right economists argued that benefit levels for the unemployed were too close to the wages of lower paid workers, thus reducing or removing the incentive to work. Some went as far as blaming most unemployment on this factor (Minford, 1983). The combination of overlapping entitlements to income-related benefits also faced low paid families with a major disincentive to work because benefits were withdrawn as fast as families increased their incomes — an effective tax rate of over 100 per cent in some cases.

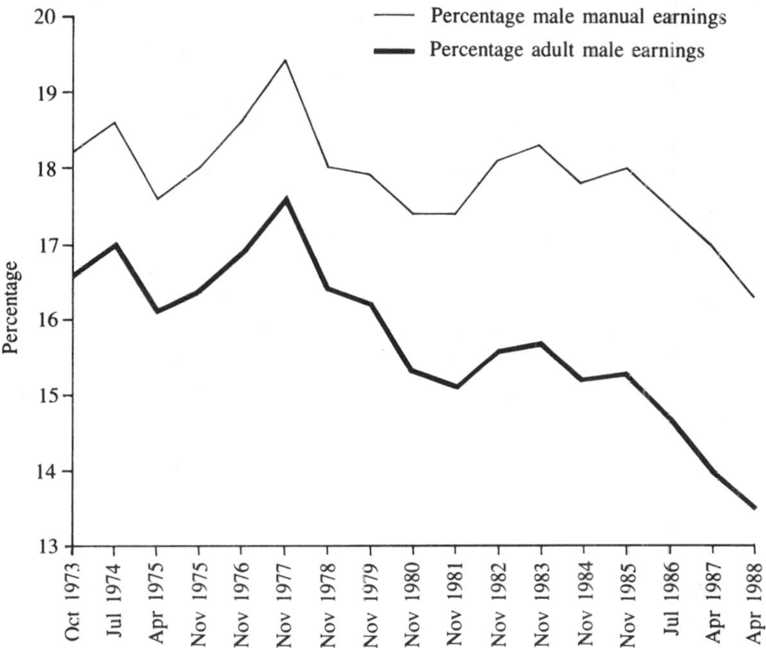

Figure 3.2 UK unemployment benefit standard rate: as percentage of average male earnings (*Source: The State of Welfare*, Hills, 1990)

There was common agreement from left and right that this 'poverty trap', as British analysts call it, was undesirable, so the government took two steps to deal with it. First, it changed the basis of the way it calculated benefits and second, it launched a detailed review of the social security system. Ever since the late 1950s benefits had been uprated not just in line with prices but with rising general standards of living. This was broadly interpreted to mean that benefits should rise in line with average earnings. Thus real levels of basic pensions and unemployment benefit had increased two and a half times from the 1940s to the end of the 1970s, in real terms. Mrs Thatcher's government changed these rules, increasing benefits only in line with prices, and not even that in the case of child benefit. As wages in the rest of the economy rose, real benefit levels fell as a proportion of average earnings (see Figure 3.2). The unemployed were hit hardest and deliberately so. Not only was their basic benefit curtailed but it was also taxed and the income-related addition that many received in addition was removed altogether. A much sharper wedge was introduced between unemployment and work. By the late 1980s benefits were worth only about one-eighth of the average male earnings for a single person. This downward trend in the relative size of the basic benefits contributed one of the most significant reductions in what would have been the burden on the Exchequer. It laid the foundation for the government's second phase of reforms.

This review of social security was said to be 'the first overall review for 40 years' (Conservative Party, 1987). It took about two years altogether and did involve a considerable amount of rethinking and analysis. It is all the more instructive, then, that it produced a relatively marginal set of changes, at least in the short run. The original intention had been to phase out the State Earnings Related Pension Scheme (SERPS) altogether. This resembled the American social security scheme in many respects. The intention was that people should be forced to contribute a given percentage of their earnings to a private scheme. In the long run this would have discharged the state's responsibility for the elderly. This proposal ran into opposition not only from the expected poverty lobby critics, to whom the government had ceased to listen anyway, but also from the pensions industry itself. The pensions industry was not at all keen to have to cover the needs of the whole retired population. Enabling people to build on a sound basic state pension was a much securer proposition for them, just as Beveridge had foreseen. The state scheme was reduced in generosity and tax incentives were given to personal private pension schemes. The long-term effect looks like being a larger private personal pension sector and a more ragged state scheme that will drive more people into private pensions.

The complex changes to means-tested schemes that followed the review slightly reduced the sharpness of some of the income tapers. The result was to bring more people within a slightly less harsh poverty trap. The bold claims of revolutionary change gave way to a rather meaner system with no greater simplicity and some more tax advantages for the private schemes. The whole episode was a hard lesson for the radical right which it learned quickly: if you want change, drive ahead quickly with the minimum of analysis and debate and if the services fall apart in the process that is all grist to the mill and will simply demonstrate the superiority of private services in comparison. More subtly, try a two stage process: move the public services nearer to the private sector model so that at some later stage it may become easier to privatize them. This last strategy is discussed in the published musings of those who had sought to persuade the government to introduce vouchers for schools (Seldon, 1986). This strategy became a theme of Mrs Thatcher's third term.

Going for radical change

The Conservative party's election manifesto in 1987 contained several radical proposals for the social services. In the next three years social policy moved to the centre of the political stage. The manifesto proposed three major changes:

- a poll tax to finance local services;
- powers for private landlords to take over local authority, or public housing;
- powers for local schools to opt out of local authority control.

On winning the election, the government legislated these changes within a year. The poll tax was designed to make every local resident aware in the most direct and unpopular way of the cost of providing local services. The expectation was that this would make it all but impossible for local councils to spend more than the government wished them to on services such as education or social care. In fact, so unpopular was the tax, that in the first year local councils were able to increase their expenditure and blame the government for the resulting high bills. In the second year the government increased its grants to the councils to buy off political unpopularity. That too failed and the tax became an issue in the challenge to Mrs Thatcher's leadership of the Conservative Party in 1990. It helped to secure her downfall and became the first symbol of her reign to be abandoned when Mr Major became Prime Minister.

The other two measures also fell flat. No private landlords took over significant amounts of property and very few non-profit housing associations did so. Tenants themselves had bought the most desirable properties and housing associations had no desire to take on difficult estates full of very poor tenants. Similarly, in the first two years only sixty schools in the whole country opted to leave their local authorities and local Conservative councillors were almost as opposed to the idea as their Labour counterparts (Glennerster, Power and Travers, 1990).

The most revolutionary changes were not put to the electorate in 1987 at all — the proposals to reform the National Health Service. Next to the monarchy, the National Health Service has been the most popular of all British social institutions (Jowell, Witherspoon and Brook, 1989). In 1988 the results of continuous cash restraint on the National Health Service began to produce a series of embarrassing scandals in which children had to be turned away from intensive care units because of staff shortages. Mrs Thatcher began to stumble in the House of Commons several weeks running on the issue, an unusual sight, and she took a typical way out — the radical one, namely, if the National Health Service is causing problems let us see if we need it at all. A no holds barred review of health care in Britain was set up. This internal review had to report to the Prime Minister within a year.

The review was bombarded by suggestions from the radical right think-tanks on ways in which it would be possible gradually to dismantle the National Health Service and replace it with a system of private insurance with tax subsidies (Pirie and Butler, 1988). Another suggestion was that Britain should introduce health maintenance organizations on the American pattern (Goldsmith and Willetts, 1988). Indeed, one of the more surprising features of the whole debate was the extent to which the United States was taken as a model for reform by the radical right. Almost all the other evidence to the review was supportive of the National Health Service, suggesting that most of its problems sprang from underfunding. Others advocated some experimental change (Barr *et al.*, 1988) but nowhere outside the right-wing think-tanks was fundamental surgery proposed.

After several months of limited progress, according to press reports (*The Economist* seems to have been well informed throughout), the team was told it had to produce proposals within the year, or else. The more extreme ideas for privatization were dropped. The Treasury, for one no doubt, was convinced that to follow the pattern of third party private health insurance would produce the kind of explosion in health care costs that had occurred in the United States (Barr *et al.*, 1988). One remnant of those ideas remained, allegedly on the insistence of the Prime Minister, which was tax relief to individuals aged over 65 who took out private health insurance. For the rest the 'reforms' involved introducing an internal or quasi-market into the

National Health Service. The basic principle of the National Health Service was to remain, it was to be free at the point of use and funded out of taxation, but its internal organization was to be fundamentally altered. The original initiative for this approach can be traced back to a visit and a publication by Enthoven (1985) who had been a leading advocate of 'managed competition' in the United States. Instead of providing, managing and funding all the health services in an area, the District Health Authorities were to become purchasers of services. The proposals were published in a White Paper, *Working for Patients* (Department of Health, 1989) and legislated the following year. The Health Authorities would issue contracts to whichever hospitals or other providers gave the best service. This was modelled closely on the 'preferred provider' model employed by Medicare and private insurers in the United States. Health Authorities would not be obliged to use the services in their own area or buy from National Health Service providers, but could buy them from another district or from the private sector. For example, medical teams within a hospital would bid to receive the cash to undertake so many hernia operations, or to provide an on-call accident and emergency service for the area. A second and competing idea was also confusingly introduced. This, too, reflected American ideas. Family doctors, or General Practitioners as the British call them, were to be given cash with which to buy services on behalf of their patients rather like a health maintenance organization. This privilege was to be confined to the largest groups of doctors only. Despite the united opposition of all the professional groups within the National Health Service, not least the British Medical Association, and the majority opposition of public opinion, the government went ahead with the changes. What the reformers seem to have underestimated is the difference in the nature of the British and the American health care markets. In the United States with a large oversupply of hospital facilities, 40 per cent of beds being unfilled at any one time, there is some chance of genuine competition to supply services. In Britain there is a shortage of provision and the past forty years have been devoted to providing a comprehensive range of services in a single set of facilities, usually the district general hospital and other specialist facilities. Outside London the range of choice of facilities geographically available is very limited. What is more, the Treasury will keep close control over any capital expenditure however that is financed, thus ensuring that no spare capacity emerges in the state sector. There is little indication that the private sector is going to risk its capital in such a political minefield and certainly not to provide spare capacity. What most managers found themselves doing in the hectic months after the Health Service and Community Care Act 1990 became law was to make contracts with those hospitals in their areas to do what they had always done but in a rather more closely defined way. The experiment with giving cash to family doctors to buy a limited range of services from hospitals — small-scale elective surgery, out-patients' care and tests of various kinds — proved potentially much more significant in its impact, but only for a small number of doctors. This transfer of cash from the top of the system to the bottom with the purchasing power in the hands of the patients' adviser, not the provider, had potential to shift the balance of power in the direction of the consumer, but it also had the potential to make practices far more careful about whom they took on as patients.

Overall, managers' control of hospital doctors may increase. Certainly there will be widespread employment of computer analysts and hardware. The efficiency outcomes have still to be seen. Optimistic managers see the distinction between purchasers and providers as potentially important and beneficial. More cynical ones think the whole affair is more of the same with computer buttons on.

From the point of view of the radical right, the move to competitive tendering and costing, the capacity for hospitals to opt out of the local National Health Service altogether and set up as independent trusts, will move the service nearer to a private model. On some future occasion it will be easier to privatize. But the radical right has made relatively little direct headway against the principle of free state-funded health care. What it has achieved is to make the left rather more flexible on the way it thinks about the reform of the National Health Service. Perhaps the most surprising thing about the whole episode has been the vigorous defence of the National Health Service by the medical profession.

Assessing the radical right

There is no doubt that the centre of gravity of political debate has changed in the United Kingdom in the past decade and a half. The economic crisis of the mid-1970s and the actual reduction in real take home pay that occurred then created a climate that was receptive to the ideas which the radical right was advancing. Yet given the

Table 3.2 Attitudes to welfare

	Per cent of population agreeing		
	Britain	United States	West Germany
It is definitely the responsibility of government to be responsible for:			
Providing health care	86	36	54
A decent standard of living			
for old people	79	43	56
for the unemployed	45	16	24
To reduce income differences between rich and poor	48	17	28

Source: Jowell, Witherspoon and Brook, 1989.

unprecedented opportunity which the radical right had to change the face of British social policy, the actual changes that have been achieved may seem relatively small, but there have been some strategic changes of real significance.

One major change is that the steady rise in the share of the national income devoted to social policy was checked. Yet this had to happen under some government because the rise of the 1960s and early 1970s could not have continued in the face of the economic crisis that came after the oil shocks. It was a Labour government that decisively began the changes.

Another change is the shift to quasi-markets and decentralized administration, which will probably have a lasting effect, although it is not uniquely a right-wing aim and is not confined to public services. It seems a far more widespread phenomenon, sometimes associated with what sociologists have come to term 'post-Fordism'.

The proposition with which the radical right began, namely that once the self-serving and inefficient nature of public social services was exposed, public support for them would collapse, has not been borne out. One of the most striking features of public opinion in the decade of Thatcher has been the growing support expressed for devoting more tax resources to public and in particular social services. At the international level, Britain was more pro-welfare at the end of the Thatcher decade than other advanced Western nations (!) (Jowell, Witherspoon and Brook, 1989) (see Table 3.2). The principles of social citizenship adumbrated during and after the Second World War seem to have proved remarkably robust, being far more deeply embedded in the popular psyche than the critics of traditional social administration predicted at the time of crisis (Mishra, 1984).

Paradoxically, the economic restructuring that was pushed through at such a high social cost in the early years of the 1980s, could not have been achieved without the kind of basic social security framework which the 1940s had put in place. Despite the reduction in benefit levels that occurred, the welfare system did succeed in putting a safety net beneath the casualties of that terrible period. The lesson is underlined looking at the events of Eastern Europe. The new governments realize that if they are to move from a command to a market system, they require as a first priority, not a stock exchange but a scheme of unemployment benefits.

The severe stretching of the income distribution that these economic changes brought meant that original incomes earned in the market were far more unequal at the end of the 1980s than in the mid-1970s. Even after the welfare state had done its job, final incomes were, even so, more unequal than before, but they were far less unequal than would have been the case without the comprehensive welfare net. Overall, the British welfare state reduced inequality one-third more in the late 1980s than it did in the 1970s (see Table 3.3). It was, in short, far more effective an agent of redistribution after Mrs Thatcher, than before. It had to be if mass starvation was to be avoided. It stood that test.

The economic changes, mitigated though they were, still left more people poor at the end of the decade than there were at the beginning and the gap between rich and poor was greater (Department of Social Security, 1990). Greater inequality had been an explicit objective of the radical right which had claimed that incentives to work had been eroded by the narrowing of earnings differentials. The intermediate goal of greater inequality was thus achieved. Whether improved overall economic efficiency resulted is not something social scientists are likely to agree about — evidence for it is slim. The underlying rate of growth in the British economy in the 1980s returned to almost exactly the same level as it had been between 1945 and 1976. Its consumers' preferences for imported goods seemed unabated. The rich gained from Mrs Thatcher's years — the extent to which they responded with higher output is difficult to see. One set of comparative losers were public service employees whose relative earnings fell a long way behind those in comparable occupations. If common experience and economic theory tell us anything it is that

Table 3.3 The impact of welfare on equality: British income distribution before and after taxes and benefits in cash and kind, 1975 to 1987

	1975	1979	1987
Original income	43	45	52
Final income	31	32	36
Reduction in inequality*	12	13	16
Share of original income taken by:			
Bottom fifth	0.8	0.5	0.3
Top fifth	44	45	51
Share of final income after the welfare state:			
Bottom fifth	7.1	7.1	6.2
Top fifth	38	38	42

*Gini coefficients (per cent)
100 = max inequality
0 = complete equality

Source: Economic Trends, May 1990.

the relative standards in the public services will fall in that situation. Thus, for the unproven improvement in the productivity of the private sector we have traded a decline in the relative quality of the public sector schools, hospitals and other services.

So far the comparative resilience of social policy in a hostile climate has been emphasized. The other side of the coin is an extension of the last point. Individuals' expectations of the standards they expect of services of any kind has continued to rise — services such as education and health are not excluded. Private spending on education and health has continued to rise — education spending by families has risen in line with incomes while state spending has not. These frustrated consumer preferences have spilled over into the private sector. Expenditure on private schools began to rise shortly after the state began to cut spending on state schools for the first time this century. It rose most in those areas that had the lowest levels of state school spending, once income and class and other relevant variables are taken into account (Glennerster and Low, 1990). There has been an increase in the numbers of families with private health cover. The longer peoples' expectations of high standards in the public sector are frustrated, the more this drift to the private sector will take place. This 'privatization by stealth' may well prove to have been the radical right's prime achievement but it is also a risky game because it could produce a backlash in favour of improving the standards of public services and there are signs that this will be the next battle line.

In short, it is too soon to draw up a final balance sheet on the impact of Mrs Thatcher's decade. In many ways the values inherent in welfare philosophy have proved to be remarkably robust. At the same time, changes have been set in train that could steadily erode those institutions in the next decade. The continuous revolution is still in process.

4

The radical right and welfare reform in the United States

Howard Jacob Karger

In 1980 the voters elected Ronald Reagan as President of the United States. Initially a dark horse candidate, the vicissitudes of Jimmy Carter's presidency, including the hostages in Iran, high rates of inflation and unemployment, and doubts about his competence, increased Reagan's appeal to American voters. In addition, Reagan's candidacy was helped by his pleas for a return to the halcyon days of yesteryear, a largely imaginary period where hard work ensured success, self-reliance was the cornerstone of society, neighbour helped neighbour, government was unobtrusive, and social and personal values were clear and mutually agreed upon. Reagan's approach to the welfare state was rooted in the same simplistic rhetoric that propelled him into the presidency: get rid of welfare chisellers, trim bloated welfare budgets, end unnecessary and redundant programmes, stimulate self-reliance in welfare recipients, and force the slothful to work. In examining the American welfare system after eight years of Reagan, one can say that the cup is either half empty or half full. For, despite almost a decade of abuse and neglect, the American welfare state remains buoyant, if not a little waterlogged. This in itself is a testimony to the resilience of the welfare concept.

This chapter will examine the effects of Reaganism on the American welfare state, with particular emphasis on its impact upon welfare reform and poverty. It begins by examining the ideology of the radical right and its perspective on the welfare state. The causes for its ascendance in American political life are also investigated. The author then examines how the movement's philosophy was operationalized in terms of the welfare state. Lastly, this chapter will address the ways in which the radical right has attempted to redefine the social contract through welfare reform proposals, especially the Family Support Act of 1988.

The radical right and the American welfare state

The conservative domination of American political life is a long-standing tradition. The pre-eminence of conservative thought is evident if one examines American politics since the beginning of the century. Except for brief periods during the early 1900s, the 1930s, and again in the 1960s, conservative politicians such as Herbert Hoover, Dwight Eisenhower, Richard Nixon, Gerald Ford, Jimmy Carter, Ronald Reagan and George Bush have been the rule rather than the exception. In that sense, the liberal antecedents of Reaganism existed only as short blips on a historical screen. Reaganism was thus less a revolution, as his supporters argued, than a return to the mainstream of American political life. In this regard, Ramesh Mishra's comments on the links between radical right ideology and established conservative ideas in American political culture are particularly apposite; he maintains that:

> Remove the context and the associated rhetoric [of the New Right] and there is little that is new — that cannot, for example, be traced to the classical doctrines of Adam Smith (individualism and market) and Herbert Spencer (social Darwinism) . . . The combination of laissez-faire in economic matters with conservatism and authoritarianism in social issues is scarcely a novel departure in the history of conservatism, especially as it has evolved in the United States. (Mishra, 1989, p. 174)

Despite this analysis, there are contextual differences between old and new conservatism that warrant the label of a radical right. For one, traditional conservatism in the American context was more élitist, less concerned with family issues, and less consumer-centred than the radical right. Traditional conservatives valued thrift and saving over ostentatious consumption. Their philosophy and prescriptions for success were based on discipline, hard work, thrift, deferment of pleasure, and a production-oriented mentality. This stands in contradistinction to the radical right which emphasizes conspicuous consumption, immediate gratification, and the creation of fortunes through speculation and investment rather than production. In that sense, Reagan's promise of a return to traditional values was deceptive. Instead of promoting historically conservative values, he opted for liberal capitalist policies that would have appalled many turn-of-the-century capitalists.

Radical right philosophy is rooted in both a social and political context. Charles Atherton (1989) outlines five propositions that sum up this basic philosophy.

First, the radical right claims that the welfare state is paternalistic and anti-libertarian. This argument maintains that any state which has the power to shift resources from one group to another represents a form of economic tyranny. Thus, instead of the traditional liberal approach which emphasizes the rights of the poor, the radical right focuses on the rights of those coerced into subsidizing the poor.

Second, the radical right argues that the welfare state is both ineffectual and counterproductive. In *Losing Ground*, Charles Murray (1984) argues that the entire federal welfare system, Aid to Families with Dependent Children (AFDC), Medicaid, Food Stamps, and unemployment insurance should be abolished because it is counterproductive and inimical to the social good.

Third, the radical right argues that the welfare state is too expensive and its results are spurious. Conservatives assert that even during the late 1960s, when massive fiscal resources were allocated to welfare programmes, social problems actually grew worse. Moreover, conservatives question whether the results of welfare programmes justify the expenditure of 17 per cent of the GNP of the United States.

Fourth, the radical right believes that the welfare state is based on faulty principles of social engineering. They fear that this kind of social engineering leads to centralized planning and eventually to a managed economy. The social welfare state is therefore seen as a precursor to fully fledged socialism.

Lastly, the welfare state is viewed by many conservatives as having lost sight of basic American values (Gilder, 1981). According to these critics, the welfare state has failed to reinforce the work ethic; the goal of self-sufficiency, self-support, and self-initiative; the importance of intact families (Mead, 1985); the fiscal responsibility of the parent to the child; and the notion of reciprocity — the idea that recipients have a social obligation to perform in return for receiving assistance. It was this conservative perspective, the desire to return to traditional values, that led in part to Reagan's electoral victory.

The ascendance of the American radical right

The welfare state experienced dramatic growth in the 1960s as a result of a basically sound and growing economy. However, the liberal consensus that guided the American welfare state since the end of the Second World War began to disintegrate in the wake of the economic slowdown of the 1970s (Mishra, 1989; Blau, 1989). The recession of the 1970s seemed to confirm what the radical right had been saying all along: the size, scope, and comprehensiveness of the welfare state was a major burden which drained society of vital investment capital through high levels of taxation. Moreover, the welfare state ruptured social cohesiveness by encouraging a strong dependence on welfare state programmes.

If conservatives reaped the harvest of the economic stagnation of the 1970s, liberals helped prepare the ground. Charles Schultze (1977), a senior fellow at the Brookings Institution and former chairman of President Carter's Council of Economic Advisers, argued that governmental intervention, through higher expenditures and increased regulation, was inferior to market strategies in dealing with social problems. Henry Aaron (1978), another Brookings senior fellow, published a critique of the 'war on poverty', concluding that the intellectual basis of poverty programmes was inherently flawed. Analysts from the liberal Urban Institute (Fisk, Kiesling and Muller, 1978) published *Private Provision of Public Services*, a programmatic evaluation of non-governmental activities in several areas, including social welfare. Thus, some of the groundwork had already been laid by liberal scholars when William Baroody, Jr (1982), then president of the conservative American Enterprise Institute, stated his intention to promote a new post-New Deal philosophy focusing on reduced governmental involvement in domestic policy.

The support for conservative initiatives came not only from intellectuals linked to the established power structure, but also from a large constituency of blue- and white-collar workers. By the late 1970s the political and social agenda of the radical right enjoyed wide support. This phenomenon occurred for a number of reasons. First, many traditional middle-class workers were sliding into a lower standard of living as a result of decreased or stagnant real incomes, high levels of underemployment and unemployment, and an increase in single-parent families (Day, 1989; Karger and Stoesz, 1990). These workers grasped at the issue of lower taxes in a desperate attempt to shore up their eroded standard of living (Wilensky, 1975). Second, stereotypes of 'welfare cheats' and large numbers of subsidized poor 'living off the fat of the land' flourished as a result of the physical and social isolation of the poor. Third, liberal affirmative action programmes, often associated with the social welfare state, became a dreaded symbol for many middle-class whites precariously holding on to their social and economic standing. Lastly, many radical right supporters had always lived in a welfare state and took its benefits and privileges for granted. These people had little idea of life outside of the protective umbrella of the welfare state.

Although initial public support for cutting welfare programmes seemed strong, the radical right soon discovered the support to be soft. When faced with the prospect of actually losing the protection of the welfare state, a number of conservative supporters — especially those in the working class — began to rethink their position. The retreat of the working class from Draconian welfare cuts was abetted by Reagan's proposals to cut middle-income social programmes, such as student, small business, and housing loans; and Medicaid (which pays for the majority of nursing home costs). It seems that some supporters of welfare cuts preferred the rhetoric to the remedy.

From theory to programme: operationalizing the radical right approach

Flushed by electoral victory, Reagan tried to fulfil his campaign promises by substantially cutting welfare expenditures, developing stringent regulations to limit coverage, and by making proposals to cut entitlement and social insurance programmes. In Reagan's bold and punishing budget cuts of 1981, AFDC funding was reduced by 11.7 per cent and stiffer eligibility requirements were enacted. The Food Stamp programme was reduced by 18.8 per cent (other food programmes were reduced by 13.3 per cent), and strikers and students became ineligible for benefits. The duration of unemployment insurance was reduced by thirteen weeks (Day, 1989). As a result of budget cuts and other fiscal policies, the poverty rate in 1984 climbed to 15.3 per cent, higher than any year since the early 1960s (Karger and Stoesz, 1990).

Radical right strategists began to realize several things in the aftermath of the 1981 budget cuts. For one, they realized that welfare programmes were not bloated and thus could not be substantially trimmed. The major welfare programmes, most of which had been fiscally neglected even before Reagan, were at their breaking point. Realizing that further cuts would have toppled an already shaky system, Reagan moderated his attacks on the welfare state. Conservatives also began to understand the resilience and hidden support for the welfare state, especially for programmes affecting the middle class.

Recognizing that deeper cuts in welfare programmes would likely destroy them, and acknowledging the tacit support given to the welfare state by the middle class (at least when it was perceived as being in danger of collapsing), Reagan was forced to consider alternative strategies. Whether by conspiracy or chance, Reagan was able to attenuate the welfare state not by direct cuts, but by creating the largest US federal budget deficit in American history.

The scope of the federal budget deficit is difficult to grasp. While the 1989 GNP of the United States was $5 trillion, the budget deficit was rapidly approaching $3 trillion. In other words, the federal budget deficit equalled three-fifths of the entire GNP in 1989. In 1988 the world traded a total of $2.7 trillion worth of goods, less than the $2.83 trillion US federal budget deficit in the third quarter of 1989. Broken down, the federal debt exceeds over $13,000 for every man, woman, and child in the United States. By creating an enormous debt (from about $50 billion a year in the Carter term to between $145 to $200 billion a year in the 1980s), the Reagan economic legacy paralyzed the growth of public services well into the next century. This federal debt has made the creation of new fiscal-based social welfare programmes almost inconceivable in the near future, regardless of emerging social problems.

Several major changes occurred as a result of the budget cuts of the early 1980s and the overall fiscal policies of the Reagan administration. For one, the current poverty rate of around 13 per cent (32 million people) is the highest since the mid-1960s. In 1978 the poverty rate stood at 11.4 per cent, with an unemployment rate of almost 11 per cent. By 1986 the poverty rate was 14.4 per cent, but the unemployment rate had dropped to 6 per cent (Karger and Stoesz, 1990). Thus, poverty in the United States does not respond to labour market conditions as it did earlier, which suggests that many of the current poor may be impervious to the ebb and flow of economic life. In other words, there seems to be a growing *lumpenproletariat* that remains poor despite the prevailing economic conditions in America.

Second, during the eight years of Reagan's presidency there was a virtual arrest in the growth of the welfare state — no major social welfare programmes were initiated and the existing ones operated on inadequate budgets. As a result, even though poverty rates increased from 1978 to 1984, AFDC rolls dropped, from 11.4 million recipients in 1975 to 10.6 million in 1984. Moreover, AFDC benefits have not kept pace with inflation, having fallen over 31 per cent in the typical state from 1970 to 1987. At present, two-thirds of the eligible poor receive no AFDC benefits, and more than half the eligible poor neither get Food Stamps nor Medicaid coverage (Karger and Stoesz, 1990).

Third, during the Reagan administration income inequality grew at an unprecedented rate. While the yearly earnings of the top 20 per cent of American families rose (after adjusting for inflation) more than $9,000 (to almost $85,000), the income of the bottom 20 per cent dropped by $576 (to $8,800) (Friedrich, 1990). The gap between the lowest and highest income brackets is the largest ever recorded by the Census Bureau (Karger and Stoesz, 1990).

Despite his public posturing, Reagan was not able to dismantle any of the major components of the welfare state. Apart from some erosion, the fundamental programmes and services of the American welfare state remained intact. The real success of the radical right, however, did not occur in budget cuts, but in its ability to undermine the ideological tenets of traditional welfare statism. In many ways the movement's success reached its apex in the Family Support Act of 1988, the first attempt at comprehensive welfare reform since the early 1970s.

Redefining the social contract: the Family Support Act of 1988

AFDC is a linchpin in the maze of federal income maintenance programmes. While its ostensible purpose is to reduce poverty (especially among children), to promote family stability, and to encourage mothers and fathers to be gainfully employed, it has been a persistent focus of controversy for many years. Despite the modest resources allocated to AFDC (less than $20 billion per year), it has become a symbol of the public's distrust of social welfare programmes.

Most presidents since John F. Kennedy have either put forward welfare proposals, or at least, given lip service to the need for reform. For example, the Work Incentive Program (WIN) was introduced in 1967 and became mandatory in 1971. WIN called for AFDC benefits to be linked to participation in job training or job search activities, but because of inadequate funding it was never implemented on a wide-scale basis. In 1971 President Richard Nixon made a bold proposal to replace AFDC and much of the income maintenance programmes with a negative income tax. Nixon's Family Assistance Plan was defeated because of Congress's scepticism and its failure to agree on an income floor.

During the past thirty years three basic approaches have been developed to reform the AFDC programme. The first strategy calls for stricter welfare eligibility and lower benefit levels to encourage recipients to choose work over welfare voluntarily. The second approach emphasizes transforming AFDC entitlement into a 'bargain', whereby grants hinge on a recipient's reciprocal obligation to accept a job, search for work, or participate in a work training programme. The third strategy focuses on alternatives to AFDC grants, including child support enforcement, changes in tax policy that reward work, and the provision of job training (Gueron, 1987).

Until recently, welfare reform had a liberal connotation since reform proposals usually called for expanding the scope, benefits, and eligibility of welfare programmes. However, by the 1980s the liberal orientation to welfare reform was eclipsed by a conservative vision. Prior to the 1970s, conservative thought held that business activity and government programmes were essentially independent of one another. Accordingly, conservatives seemed content to snipe at welfare programmes, reserving their attention for areas more in line with traditional conservative concerns: the economy, defence, and foreign affairs. By the mid-1970s, conservative intellectuals realized that social welfare activities were too important to be dismissed outright (Karger and Stoesz, 1990). Using this new window of opportunity, a radical right-wing position was formulated which sought to contain the growth in governmental welfare programmes and to transfer as much federal welfare responsibility as possible to states and the private sector (Steinfels, 1979).

This conservative position was based on several ideological tenets, including a deep antagonism toward governmental involvement in social welfare programmes. Government programmes were faulted for a breakdown in the mutual obligation between groups, the lack of attention to efficiencies and incentives in the way programmes are operated and benefits awarded, the induced dependency of beneficiaries on programmes, and the growth of the welfare industry and its special interest groups, particularly professional associations (Karger and Stoesz, 1990).

Based on these ideological predilections, conservative scholars began to develop plausible proposals for welfare reform, including serious proposals in the areas of workfare, community development, and child welfare (Rabushka, 1980; Anderson, 1980; Gilder, 1981; Meyer, 1981; Murray, 1984; Butler and Kondratas, 1987; Novak, 1987; Lind and Marshner, 1987). Within a short period, the liberal hegemony in social welfare was confronted by a group of scholars who held a vastly different view of the limits, scope and responsibilities of the American welfare state.

The conservative critique of social welfare contained several general objectives, including undercutting the welfare state by limiting the discussion of 'welfare' to means-tested programmes, thereby segregating them from the more popular social insurance programmes. Secondly, radical right supporters attempted to lessen the role of the federal government in domestic social policy by assigning more responsibility for welfare to the states as well as the private for-profit and non-profit sectors. This successful strategy resulted in an increase in the fragmentation of welfare programmes as well as an erosion of the ideological underpinnings of the American welfare state (Karger and Stoesz, 1990).

Welfare reform proposals were made during the presidential administrations of Jimmy Carter and Ronald Reagan. Both proposals, which were similar, included some form of mandatory work obligation and both called for a redefinition of welfare entitlement. Moreover, both proposals suggested that the right to receive welfare benefits should be linked with the obligation to work. Apart from these similarities there were also important differences. For example, the Carter proposal would have guaranteed recipients full-time, paid public service jobs. The Reagan plan called for universal 'workfare' whereby recipients would have to work in the private sector in exchange for their welfare cheques. Congress rejected Carter's Programme for

Better Jobs and Income because of its annual price tag of $15 billion. On the other hand, major parts of the Reagan programme were incorporated into the Family Support Act of 1988.

The new welfare reform initiative

The Family Support Act of 1988 was a compromise bill which came out of a conservative Congress operating under a huge federal budget deficit. Although conservative, the Family Support Act appeared moderate in the light of proposals coming from the Reagan White House. For example, an earlier proposal made by the Reagan administration, the Low-Income Opportunity Act, would have effectively eliminated a poor mother's entitlement to support from federal welfare programmes. This proposals would have given states wide latitude in programme design, eligibility guidelines, benefit levels, and the allocation of programme resources. In essence, the Reagan proposal called for a series of state-sponsored welfare experiments with virtually no assistance from the federal government.

Differences between a moderately conservative Democratic plan and the very conservative Reagan proposal were ironed out in a compromise bill which Representative Thomas Downey, Chair of the House Subcommittee on Public Assistance, hailed as the first 'significant change in our welfare system in 53 years' (Eaton, 1988, p. 15). Under this bill, $3.34 billion is to be allocated over the first five years for states to establish education and job-seeking programmes for AFDC recipients. During 1990 and 1991 states will have to enrol at least 7 per cent of AFDC parents in 'workfare', and by 1995, the mandatory enrolment will rise to 20 per cent. Although the AFDC unemployed parent programme (covering two-parent families) was made mandatory for all states, beginning in 1977 one parent will be required to work at least 16 hours a week in an unpaid job in exchange for benefits (Rich, 1988). Among the more progressive provisions of the bill are the extension of eligibility for day-care grants and Medicaid for one year after leaving AFDC. This bill also mandates the automatic deduction of child support from an absent parent's pay cheque. Representative Dan Rostenkowski, Chair of the House Ways and Means Committee (which oversees most welfare legislation), estimated that an additional 65,000 two-parent families would receive benefits, that 400,000 people would participate in workfare by 1993, and that 475,000 people would be eligible for transitional Medicaid benefits under provisions of the bill (Rich, 1988). The Family Support Act was signed into law by President Reagan on 15 October 1988.

Problems in the Family Support Act of 1988

The Family Support Act represents a triumph of style over substance. While several provisions of this bill will help parents who have work skills, the majority of people on AFDC exhibit a job history in which welfare complements episodic and low-wage employment. Thus, while the new welfare reform initiative will extend benefits to the working poor, it is unlikely to remove most people from welfare. Judith Gueron, an authority on workfare, notes that:

> . . . although the programs [work/welfare initiatives] produced changes, the magnitude of those changes was relatively modest . . . . Thus, while it is worthwhile to operate these programs, they will not move substantial numbers of people out of poverty. (Gueron, 1987, p. 29)

The Family Support Act also contains other structural problems. For one, it assumes that the economy is capable of producing large numbers of well-paid jobs. Although 20 million new jobs were created in the 1980s, they were not with the *Fortune 500* companies, who cut their workforces by 3.5 million. Many of the new jobs produced in the 1980s were low-paying service positions in the secondary labour market (Friedrich, 1990). Moreover, high-paid manufacturing jobs declined the most during the 1980s, and poverty in the traditional industrial states went up accordingly. In Pennsylvania, New Jersey, and New York the poverty rates climbed from 10.4 per cent in 1978 to 13.4 per cent in 1985; in Michigan, Ohio and Illinois they went up from 10 per cent to 14 per cent. Permanent job losses in Ohio include a 20 per cent loss in primary metals manufacturing, a 10 per cent loss in electronic equipment manufacturing, and a 19 per cent loss in transportation equipment manufacturing. Between 1970 and 1982 the number of high-income production jobs declined by 1.4 million (Day, 1989). These data illustrate that welfare recipients who are expected to become self-sufficient through the labour market, will not easily find jobs in the relatively well-paid industrial sector — an area which previously allowed for economic mobility. Recipients will therefore have to concentrate on finding employment in the low-paid secondary labour market, a niche which does not encourage economic self-sufficiency. In short, the working poor will continue to need substantial welfare benefits unless wages increase and jobs are made more reliable.

Second, key provisions of the welfare reform bill are punitive and unlikely to enhance the economic self-sufficiency of AFDC recipients. Requiring one parent of two-parent households to do make-work in exchange for benefits will not increase economic independence; instead, forced work may actually impede self-sufficiency if beneficiaries are forced to do make-work instead of seeking real work in the labour market.

Third, garnishing wages of the non-custodial parent is unlikely to increase the economic independence of many female-headed households or of low-paid male workers. In fact, garnishing wages of low-paid male workers can create a disincentive to work. Mimi Abramovitz observed that for poor men this provision 'may be more like squeezing blood from a stone' (Abramovitz, 1988, p. 239).

Fourth, expecting states to operate inadequately funded workfare programmes may result in uneven welfare reform. For example, wealthy states such as Massachusetts and California will expand on already generous workfare programmes, while poor states such as Mississippi and New Mexico, will likely institute narrow and punitive workfare programmes.

Fifth, the current welfare reform bill does not ameliorate the long-standing erosion of cash grants to poor families. AFDC benefits currently remain below the poverty level for all states, except Alaska (Committee on Ways and Means, 1988). From 1970 to 1988, the median state's AFDC benefit dropped 35 per cent (in constant dollars) as a result of inflation. In other words, if AFDC benefits had kept up with inflation, beneficiaries in 1988 would have received an additional $5.88 billion. The 1988 welfare reform bill will redistribute to the poor only 57 per cent of this lost income ($3.34 billion) over a five year span. Moreover, even this inadequate reallocation will be diluted by channelling it through a compulsory workfare programme (Karger and Stoesz, 1990).

Sixth, the new welfare reform bill fails to tackle one of the most serious problems in AFDC — the lack of a national AFDC benefit standard. Specifically, this bill does not rectify a system which allows states such as Alabama, Kentucky, Louisiana, Mississippi, Tennessee and Texas to award a family of three an AFDC grant of less than

$200 per month (Karger and Stoesz, 1990). (In comparison, Alaska, California, Vermont and Connecticut pay the same family over $600 per month.)

The welfare reform bill is flawed in another way. In November 1987, there were 7.1 million poor workers, many of whom worked full-time. Between 1978 and 1987 the number of working poor climbed by nearly 2 million, or 23 per cent; the poor who worked full-time and year round climbed by 43 per cent (Reich, 1989). Nearly 60 per cent of the 20 million people who fall below the Census Bureau's poverty line are from families with at least one member in full- or part-time work. If 7 million workers are unable to achieve economic self-sufficiency, how can welfare recipients be expected to become completely independent of public assistance? Moreover, even though unemployment has dropped to less than 6 per cent, it is differentially distributed. Relatively well-off sections of the country (e.g., Massachusetts, New Hampshire and California) experience low unemployment, while the 'rust bowl' of the industrial midwest and the farm states experience high rates of unemployment. Furthermore, unemployment rates may differ widely even within states. Vigorous promotion of workfare may thus force poor rural families to move to urban areas for job possibilities, a trend that will adversely affect already unstable rural areas.

For the poor, the welfare reform bill of 1988 represents little more than regaining a small portion of the AFDC benefits lost since 1970. Moreover, there is little in 'welfare reform' that represents a significant improvement in the lives of impoverished families. Nevertheless, three fundamental values emerge from the largely symbolic Family Support Act of 1988: reciprocity, productivity, and familial responsibility.

Reciprocity

Some social welfare theorists insist that welfare programmes contribute to dependency and dysfunctional behaviours, especially when benefits are not linked to an expected standard of conduct. Charles Murray (1984) maintains that the very system designed to help the poor has created dependency by penalizing the virtuous and rewarding the dysfunctional. In a compelling argument, Lawrence Mead observes that:

> . . . the damage [by welfare programmes] seems to be done, not by the benefits, themselves, but by the fact that they are *entitlements*, given regardless of the behaviour of clients. They raise the income

> of recipients, but, more important, free them to behave without accountability to society. (Mead, 1985, p. 65)

Although reciprocity is promoted as a way to encourage socially desirable behaviour in welfare recipients, it also contributes to the public credibility of welfare programmes. In introducing his welfare reform proposal (which included a workfare component), Daniel Patrick Moynihan argued:

> Mothers, the custodial parents in most single-parent families, must try to earn income, at least part-time, to help support their children. The statistics are a stark testament to the need: 72 per cent of all mothers with children between 6 and 18 are in the labour force. Over half of all mothers with children under age 3 are in the labour force.
>
> This marks a great change in the position of women in American life. The only women who have not participated in this change are the heads of AFDC families, of whom fewer than 5 per cent work part-time or full-time. As a nation, we find a 7 per cent unemployment rate barely tolerable. What then are we to think of a system that keeps 95 per cent of poor mothers unemployed and out of the labour force? (Moynihan, 1987, pp. S10401–2)

A study of five workfare experiments by the Manpower Demonstration Research Corporation found that the most dependent AFDC recipients — those with no pre-assistance earnings and on public assistance for more than two years — showed the greatest gains from participation in workfare. In other words, targeting workfare on the more problematic welfare clients can result in greater savings than focusing on AFDC recipients who possess more employment assets and are thus more likely to become independent of AFDC (Gueron, 1988). In conditions of restricted funding, workfare administrators may choose cost reduction over economic independence, thus leaving workfare vulnerable to accusations that the programme has not significantly reduced the AFDC caseload (Freidlander, 1988). In the end, the inadequate funding of the Family Support Act may subvert its very purpose.

Productivity

The United States is being forced to consider new ways to utilize its labour force more effectively as a result of its immersion into a highly competitive global economy, where Asian and other competitors exploit their productive capacity more fully. Given the new economic realities, the ascendance of conservative values, and the severe budgetary restraints, the federal government is likely to force social programmes to become more congruent with economic productivity.

Within this context, welfare programmes can be used to rebuild deteriorating American communities. The precedent exists with the jobs programmes of the New Deal — the Civilian Conservation Corps, the Works Progress Administration, the Public Works Administration — and more recent examples, such as the California Conservation Corps. The redefinition of relief from an emphasis on welfare to one on work, holds the promise of using social programmes to reconstruct America's deteriorating infrastructure. Allying welfare with productivity also draws social programmes closer to the American economic system, a strategy that may be necessary to justify future social welfare expenditures.

Familial responsibility

Another ideological premise reflected in the current welfare reform bill is the belief that government should abandon its role as the 'rescuer of first resort'. Retreating to traditional values, this philosophy dictates that biological parents have the ultimate responsibility to support their offspring.

Although even impoverished non-custodial parents have been required to pay child support since 1981, the 1988 AFDC reforms call for even more stringent enforcement. While automatic withholding of child support payments will clearly keep some families off AFDC, it is limited when applied universally. Current research suggests that the typical child support situation involves a man who is remarried and whose income can provide some economic support for his biological children. However, the record for child support enforcement is bleak. In 1986 child support collections were successful in only 15.7 per cent of AFDC cases (Greene, 1987). Perhaps more a principle than a fiscal attempt to gain revenue, this policy reinforces the traditional belief in the responsibility of the parent to physically provide for the child.

Conclusion: the achievement of the radical right

While the radical right can rightfully claim major successes in reshaping American social welfare policy during the 1980s, its most important achievement has been in creating a far-reaching conservative ambience. An example of the social policy success of the radical right is illustrated by the Family Support Act. In contrast to ambitious proposals advanced by previous administrations, the welfare reform bill of 1988 was comparatively modest. Even groups previously enraged by Reagan's strikes against welfare, such as the National Governors' Association and the American Public Welfare Association, reacted to the conservative *Zeitgeist* and supported a bill that was conservative in contrast to those of the past.

At present, the social, economic, and political forces that have propelled the radical right appear likely to influence social policy well into the next century. In that context, the Family Support Act of 1988 does not simply reflect a benign policy initiative; instead, it represents a fundamental shift away from sweeping notions of universal entitlements toward a strongly residual formulation of social welfare. Welfare reform ideologies that stress reciprocity, productivity, and familial responsibility represent a return to traditional values of self-reliance, independence, individual responsibility, and the limited role of government. For liberals who advocate expanding social welfare programmes, this bill represents a deterioration of the traditional liberal consensus.

Regional and international economic developments can pose significant problems for government. When economic events displace large numbers of workers, it becomes the government's responsibility to sweep up the social debris. From this perspective, a conservative ideology of welfare reform is not only out of step with a post-industrial economy, it also condemns individuals for their impoverishment and their inability to compete successfully in the marketplace.

In many ways, the current welfare reform bill represents a legislative sleight-of-hand. With modest funding (less than $3.5 billion over a five year period), the likelihood that this bill will significantly change the welfare system is remote. The adroitness of this bill, however, lies in its ability to exchange illusion for reality, a hallmark of both New Right ideology and the Reagan era.

5

The Chicago Boys, social security and welfare in Chile

Silvia Borzutzky

Since the early twentieth century social security and welfare policies have occupied a prominent role in Chile's socioeconomic and political system. Their importance explains not only the early development of a large and complex social security system but also the comprehensive changes to the system implemented by the government of General Augusto Pinochet in the 1980s.

This chapter discusses Chile's social security system which includes the pension and family allowances systems, health protection and a system of workman's compensation. It will focus on the birth of the system in 1924, its evolution and impact, and the changes implemented in the 1980s which entailed the application of a set of (radical or *New Right*) monetarist economic principles. The change to the pension system is unique since it involved its almost total privatization, followed by the partial privatization of health and workman's compensation.

Chile's political and economic history: a brief summary

Before the 1973 coup, Chile stood out among the Latin American countries because of its strong democratic institutions and its stable political system. Chile's political stability can be traced back to a number of social and political factors which include the early institutionalization of the country in the 1830s, the integration of the land-owning and industrial classes into a coherent sociopolitical force and the belief among the élite in an organized, legitimate, form of government.

The enactment of the 1925 constitution involved the incorporation of a set of democratic principles including a presidential system in which congress retained a large degree of power, the establishment of the universal right to vote for men, and the legalization of a multiparty political system which soon included parties ranging from the conservatives in the right to the communists in the left.

Chile's presidential democracy rested in a complex legislative process which balanced and checked the powers of the two main branches of government. While this structure facilitated political accommodation and provided a basis for political stability, it also contributed to inefficiency and political paralysis since it forced compromise and prevented the passage of any legislation that could drastically affect the existing distribution of political and economic power (Borzutzky, 1990).

In the socioeconomic area the 1925 constitution incorporated the notion of the state as a central economic actor. The constitution involved an adaptation of ideas developed in Western Europe during the nineteenth century which gave the state a central role in rapidly industrializing and changing societies. Following the French constitutionalist Leon Duguit among others, who argued that the state function was to provide for public needs, the constitution established that the state had both social and economic responsibilities, including the provision of health and social welfare. The expansion of the state functions in Chile between 1925 and 1973 followed precisely Duguit's ideas regarding the need for an activist state during periods of rapid social and economic changes.

In the area of social policy both the 1925 constitution and the social security legislation of 1924 were also strongly influenced by Bismarck's paternalistic approach to social policy which provided the intellectual foundations for Chile's social security and health legislation.

By the late 1960s the state had acquired a central role in the economic life of the nation, owning either totally or partially key industrial areas such as copper, steel, petrochemicals; controlling over half of the credit; setting minimum wages, prices and salaries; and controlling about 40 per cent of total GDP and over 70 per cent of the gross domestic investment (Stallings, 1978). Throughout this period the country experienced a number of economic problems which governments from both the right and the centre-left proved unable to resolve. Thus, inflation, low rate of economic growth, low rate of capital accumulation, dependency on copper and unequal distribution of income became structural elements of the Chilean economy. Among them, inflation had the most pervasive consequences since it did not only produce permanent economic dislocations, but also a sense of constant economic and political crisis which were central not only to the political and economic decisions made by the government but also central to the form in which the social security system developed.

One final element needs to be added to this summary of Chile's political and economic characteristics and that is the nature of the labour organization and its relationship with the political parties. The bases of the labour union system were set by the 1924 law which established a highly regulated union organization characterized by the division of the labour movement between blue- and white-collar workers. Plant unions were the core organizational unit of the blue-collar workers while craft unions were the central organizational unit of the white-collar worker. This legal distinction between plant and craft unions and the prohibition of the federations of unions to negotiate collective contracts constituted the main weakness of the Chilean labour movement. Needless to say that this division reflected the desire of the ruling élite to control and divide Chile's labour force.

Although the 1924 law divided the labour movement it could not prevent the transformation of the unions into important political actors. In the context of a competitive, multiparty democracy the labour movement counteracted its political weakness by developing what we have described elsewhere as a symbiotic relationship with the political parties. The parties, for their part, were eager to co-opt electoral clienteles and to represent the interests of the different sectors of the labour movement in congress (Angell, 1973; Pizarro, 1978).

The relationship between the labour movement and the political system is essential to understand the development of the social security system between 1925 and 1973. This relationship has to be analyzed at two different levels. At a national level the leftist parties developed strong linkages with the Marxist-oriented Confederation of Workers, or CUT, while at a different level each union or sectors within the working class developed a relationship with a member or group of members of a political party. This brokerage function was exercised by politicians of all colours and among its many consequences was the piecemeal expansion of the functions of the state and the passage of a mass of particularistic social legislation devoted to protect specific groups within the working class.

The Chilean social security system: 1924–73

The development of Chile's social security system during this period reflects the competitive nature of the political system and the urgent socioeconomic problems that affected the majority of the population. Two crucial elements need to be highlighted here: first, the nature of the 1924 laws that set the bases for Chile's social security legislation and, second, the growth of the system between the mid-1930s until the early 1970s.

Before 1924 Chile's social legislation was formed by a few isolated laws. The first Worker's Accidents Law dates from 1916 and is important because it established the employer's obligation of discharging the burden of proof. In 1917, a nursery law obligated the employer to maintain a nursery in industries employing more than fifty women, while in 1918 the first pension fund was established.

In 1924, in the midst of a military action geared to force the renewal of a paralyzed political system, Chile's congress approved the law 4054 which established a compulsory blue-collar worker's pension system, as well as laws dealing with the formation of unions and with the right to strike (Morris, 1966). Originally, the law established only old age pensions for those 65 years or older, invalidity pensions and illness and maternity benefits. The following year, under a temporary military government, four new funds were created: the Civil Servants' Fund, the White-Collar Workers' Fund, the Armed Forces Fund and the Police Fund. Common to all the funds were the principles of employers' and employees' contributions, and administration of the funds by a body formed by representatives of the state, of the insured and led by a board of directors appointed by the President of the Republic.

From the beginning the insured population was divided along occupational lines and, also, from the beginning each of the funds received different types of benefit. Through the years the basic five funds remained the same but a dynamic evolved according to which small subgroups separated themselves from the basic funds and obtained the legislative approval needed to create special funds that offered more and better benefits. In other cases the group stayed within the fund, but obtained special privileges. This process of dismemberment of the social security system resulted in the creation of about 160 different funds, and a legal labyrinth of about '1600 laws, decrees, and regulations [which] remained uncompiled and uncoordinated' (Mesa Lago, 1978). By 1973 the number of social security laws was more than 2,000.

In general, the system provided four major types of benefits: pensions, family allowances, health and maternity benefits, and cash benefits. The nature and quality of the benefits was determined by one's affiliation to a fund or group within a fund. It is impossible to provide a detailed description of the benefits associated with a given fund or group since we know that there were about 2,200 different systems of benefits (Comisión de Estudios, 1965). In the area of pensions the systems provided a wide array of old age and disability pensions to all occupational groups, while special pensions based on years of service were offered to civil servants and some white-collar workers. The conditions required to obtain a pension and the amount received changed from group to group.

The financial structure was based on the principle of employers, workers and state contributions for the blue-collar workers, and a system of employers' and employees' contributions for the civil servants and white-collar workers, but contributions ranged widely in all systems (Briones, 1968). As benefits expanded a new financial modality appeared: the establishment of special taxes earmarked to finance specific social security benefits for a special group. Moreover, improvements in the benefits received by public employees also increased the fiscal commitment to the system since these benefits required additional resources.

By 1970, Chile had a comprehensive, but regressive pension system. The system provided benefits to 69.5 per cent of the economically active population or 68.6 per cent of the total population (Mesa Lago, 1978) which made it one of the most comprehensive systems in Latin America. However, as several studies have indicated, the social security had a negative impact on income distribution. Among them, Mesa Lago concluded that of the four main groups the armed forces contributed least to their own system, followed by the blue-collar workers, the white-collar workers and the civil servants (Mesa Lago, 1978).

The family allowances programme represented about 50 per cent of the system's expenditures and covered 73.2 per cent of the population. By and large the benefits were financed by a 22 per cent tax paid by the employer. During the Frei administration (1964–70) the programme was reformed and some of its most important inequities were eliminated through increases in the allowances received by the lowest income groups and by enforcing the application of the law in the countryside (Borzutzky, 1982).

Since 1925, health protection was intimately linked to the social security system. Law 4054 of 1925 established that those insured by the blue-collar workers' fund had the right to receive medical attention and a subsidy in case of illness and maternity. In 1938, law 6178 established the obligation of all the insurance funds to create preventive medical services and to provide subsidies to those suffering from one of the designated illnesses. These benefits and services were financed by a 1 per cent wage tax paid by the employer. The application of these laws produced an improvement in the dismal health standards of the population at that time (Bustos, 1946).

In order to comply with the laws, the five major funds created comprehensive medical services for their affiliates, including hospitalization. The most important of these services was the National Health Service (SNS) created in 1952 with the purpose of providing medical attention to blue-collar workers and indigents and of performing general public health functions. The functions of the National Health Service were financed by the blue-collar workers' fund, which contributed 4.5 per cent of its revenue to the National Health Service, and by the state.

The establishment of the National Health Service was followed by the creation of the National Employees Medical Services (or SERMENA), which provided care to white-collar workers and civil servants. Prior to 1968 SERMENA provided only preventive care, but after 1968 its functions were expanded to curative medicine as well.

In the area of workman's compensations the financial responsibility fell entirely on the employer and the programmes were administered not by funds, but by insurance companies.

By the mid-1960s the administration of the different social security programmes was charged to hundreds of agencies which not only augmented the costs of the system, but also created administrative chaos. This, in turn, was the result of the dismemberment of the five original funds into hundreds of funds. In the long run this process led to a destruction of the notion of social solidarity and created an enormous financial burden on the state. In the mid-1960s social security revenues amounted to 12.2 per cent of GNP while expenditures were equal to 8.2 per cent of GNP (Mesa Lago, 1978).

The social security system's anarchic and discriminatory structure can be attributed to the divisionary and exclusionary nature of the labour legislation passed in 1924 and 1925 which forced the multiple units that formed the working class to develop clientelistic relations with the political parties. The parties, in turn, offered the workers state-financed benefits in return for political support. Given Chile's persistent inflation and a very unequal distribution of income, these policies became essential to the existence of the political system and even the notion of reforming them encountered massive opposition.

In fact, since the mid-1950s every president had argued in favour of a thorough reform of the system. President Jorge Alessandri (1958–64) went as far as creating a special commission charged with the task of studying the current system and proposing a reform. The commission, known as the Prat Commission, produced a crude assessment of the system and a set of recommendations, but the administration lacked the political will to follow up the recommendations. In 1965 President Frei made public his commitment to reform and announced his intentions to reform all aspects of the social security and health system (Frei, 1965). The Christian Democratic administration moved both in the administrative and in the legislative fronts; administratively by trying to obtain full compliance with existing laws and by increasing the benefits received by the lowest income groups, and legislatively by introducing to congress bills that aimed at reforming the pension system and expanding curative medicine.

In the final analysis the administration succeeded in implementing a number of administrative reforms such as the expansion of medical services to rural areas, improvements in the family allowances received by the poorest income groups, and enforcement of the laws in the countryside where, traditionally, the landowners had managed to ignore the labour and social security legislation (Loveman, 1977). But the existing distribution of power made it impossible for President Frei to carry out a complete legislative reform of the pension system since all political parties including even sectors of his own party opposed such reform since it damaged the interests of core constituencies of the parties.

By 1970, when President Allende came to power both the political system and the social security system were at the brink of a major crisis; the crisis unfolded between 1970 and 1973. The programme of Allende's Popular Unity coalition emphasized the need to provide universal social security coverage as well as health services to the entire population creating in Chile a welfare state in which everybody received the same type of benefits and was entitled to full medical care, all financed through direct taxes (Allende, 1972). In practice, the government only achieved an expansion of coverage which benefited several groups of independent workers and which expanded the population covered to 76 per cent of the economically active population. Allende also reduced the requisites needed to obtain welfare assistance, increased some of the lowest pensions, and improved the pensions received by the military and the police (Laws 17595 and 17418).

In brief, Allende's policies were not geared to obtain a total transformation of the system, but to expand it and to improve the benefits received by critical sectors such as the middle class, the military and the police. The administration did not attempt to end the existing system of unequal benefits. In the health area the Popular Unity government stressed the importance of raising the awareness of the population about their health rights, while increasing the resources devoted to the provision of health. Here, the statistics show both an increase in the demand for medical attention and a decrease in the infant mortality rate which had also declined during the Frei administration (Allende, 1972).

By 1973 both the social security system and the entire political organization were undergoing a structural crisis. The social security system suffered from an acute financial crisis produced by the continuous expansion of the benefits which imposed new obligations on the existing institutions or created new ones with total disregard for the financial impact of their policies. The political organization at large suffered from a dual process of polarization, which led to the disappearance of the political centre, and an erosion of the government's legitimacy which set the stage for the coup (Sigmund, 1977; Valenzuela, 1978).

Authoritarianism and neo-liberalism: the radical right in Chile

Chile's democratic regime and the institutions that were the trademark of the country's sociopolitical organization were destroyed in the bloody coup of 11 September 1973. In the following months and years the new government led by General Augusto Pinochet closed the congress; banned all political parties, unions and other political organizations; killed, tortured and/or exiled former political leaders. The destruction of the previous political order was followed by the need to reorganize the society along new lines. In the economic area these new lines were proposed by a group of economists trained at the Catholic University of Chile and the University of Chicago, popularly known as the Chicago Boys.

The history of the Chicago Boys in Chile dates from an exchange agreement signed in 1956 between the Catholic University of Chile and the University of Chicago, according to which the economics department of the University of Chicago should provide training to a selected group of graduate students of the Catholic University. The agreement, financed by the United States Agency for International Development, allowed 'the best and the brightest' of the students at the Catholic University to get special training at Chicago and professors from Chicago to teach their doctrines in Chile.

There are many interesting elements in this agreement that allow us to understand the process of diffusion of monetarist ideas. From the standpoint of the US government the agreement was rooted in the importance of providing technical assistance to less developed countries which, in turn, was generated by the dynamics of the cold war. Among the ideas that inspired these technical assistance projects to Latin America were the importance of training local élites for the development process, particularly economic development, and the need to maintain the Latin American economies linked to the United States and organized around capitalist economic principles. Specifically, in the case of Chile, the goals were to help Chile deal with its persistent inflation, support capitalism and free enterprise, and to develop educational institutions capable of providing adequate technological and economic training (Valdés, 1989).

From the standpoint of the economics department of the University of Chicago, which had been guided by the ideas of Milton Friedman, there was a need to expand their own ideas about underdevelopment and modernization which rejected both Keynesian economics and the development notions proposed by the Economic Commission for Latin America of the United Nations that stressed the importance of substitutive industrialization, structural reforms and a large dosage of government intervention in the economy. The Chicago economists, in turn, proposed the development of market institutions, the opening of the local economies to international competition and the development of human capital. According to one analyst, the entire programme with the Catholic University was then inspired by the need to demonstrate the applicability of the monetarist approach to underdevelopment, as well as the importance of creating a cadre of well-trained economists in a less developed country. These two primary goals were followed by the need of that department of obtaining US government funds and to increase the pool of students (Valdés, 1989).

Finally, the Chilean partner, the department of economics of the Catholic University, could only gain from the agreement. Although the Catholic University was the second largest in the country and had an excellent reputation in some areas, it had a very small department of economics with very little human or material resources. The agreement with Chicago could only enhance its resources and reputation.

The Chicago Boys, thus, were the product of this successful exchange programme. Through the years, twenty-six economists were trained at Chicago and many of them were later hired as professors at the Catholic University. Two individuals became essential in the process: Arnold Haberger, from Chicago, and Sergio de Castro. De Castro, who was one of the first students to go to Chicago and become the 'dean' of the group in Chile, led the process of transformation of the Chilean economy in the late 1970s. Haberger was the leader of the Chile project in Chicago, travelled to Chile often, married a Chilean and guided his Chilean disciples in their mission once they got policy-making duties.

Although the Chicago Boys had existed since the early 1960s, their ideas remained marginal to the economic discussion in Chile and their influence was limited to the classrooms of the Catholic University. However, with the deepening of the economic and political crisis in the early 1970s their importance grew. In August of 1972 a group of ten economists under the leadership of de Castro began to work on the formulation of an economic programme that would replace the policies implemented by the Allende administration. In fact, the existence of this plan was essential to any attempt on the part of the armed forces to overthrow Allende since the Chilean armed forces did not have any economic plan of their own. As one marine officer argued, the key issue was not how to overthrow Allende, but how to solve the economic problems of the country (Fontaine, 1988). The programme was in the hands of the military in May of 1973 and it had two objectives: first, to guide the actions of those who opposed Allende, and second, to formulate a global economic programme to be applied by a new government in the event that the Allende regime was overthrown. According to the report of the United States Senate on covert actions in Chile, the activities of these economists were financed by the Central Intelligence Agency (CIA) (United States Government, 1975).

Although the Chicago Boys, and particularly de Castro, had had a close relationship with the military since 1972, it was not until 1977 that the Chicago Boys took total control of economic policy making with the appointment of de Castro as Minister of Finance and other members of the group in the Ministries of Economics, Labour and Social Security and the National Planning Office. The process of consolidation of their power ran through 1978 and it was intimately linked with the ongoing political process.

From a political perspective, what is important to note is that the Pinochet government went through a number of stages. During the initial phase, from 1973 to 1975, the emphasis was on the elimination of all vestiges of the previous political system and the policies were based on the principles of the national security doctrine. Massive repression and the elimination of former political actors were the weapons used by the military regime in its battle against not only Marxism, but parties and politicians in general. Between 1975 and 1978 the government tried, unsuccessfully, to find a source of legitimacy other than the battle against Marxism. In 1978 it began to emphasize the subsidiary role of the state and the monetarist economic policies.

The period between 1978 and 1980 was crucial both for General Pinochet and for the monetarist economists since they all managed to consolidate their power. The central political manoeuvres were the 1978 plebiscite that gave General Pinochet total control of the executive branch and the enactment of the constitution of 1980 that legitimized the authoritarian system. At the same time the Chicago Boys, or Economic Team, as it was called in Chile, obtained full control of economic and social policies and used their power to carry out not only a total transformation of the Chilean economy, but also the entire social structure based on the principles of the market.

Few things were more foreign to Chilean society than the market ideology and the notions of individualism, competence and consumption that the ideology involves. The Chilean disciples of Milton

Friedman and Frederick von Hayek argued that the market is the only social entity capable of regulating social interaction without coercion, guaranteeing at the same time a rationally based behaviour and freedom (Brunner and Garcia, 1981; Foxley, 1981; Valdés, 1989). In the long run, the market was expected to replace the state as the regulator of economic activity and social interactions, eliminating the *raison d'être* of the state. In the meantime the authoritarian nature of the government was considered to be vital for the success of the 'neo-liberal revolution' as it was called in Chile because 'it provided a lasting regime; it gave the authorities a degree of efficiency that it was not possible to obtain in a democratic regime; and it made possible the application of a model developed by experts and that did not depend upon the social reactions produced by its implementation'. De Castro was even more explicit when he declared that the effective freedom of a person can be guaranteed only by an authoritarian government which exercises power through equal, universal norms (de Castro, 1976).

The Chicago-trained economists emphasized the scientific nature of their programme and the need to replace politics by economics and the politicians by economists. Thus, the decisions made were not the result of the will of the authority, but they were determined by their scientific knowledge. The use of the scientific knowledge, in turn, would reduce the power of the government since decisions will be made by technocrats and by the individuals in the private sector. Thus, the economists would, in the long run, return to the society the freedom that is inherent within its nature (Brunner, 1981).

Based on the principles of the market, the economic model was designed to open the entire economy to the external market and to allow the private sector to compete freely. In regard to inflation, the application of monetarist principles had already begun in 1975 with the 'shock policy' that drastically reduced government expenditures, accelerated the reduction in the size of the public sector and imposed a tight monetary policy (Cahuas, 1979). The key to the entire policy was the reduction in the size and functions of the state. The concept of the subsidiary role of the state, then, became central to the new approach, involving the notion that the state should perform only those activities that could not be performed by the private sector, either because they impinged upon the security of the country or because they involved an effort beyond the capability of the private entrepreneur. Following this principle there was a reduction of both the regulatory and direct economic functions of the state, including the privatization of 437 of the 507 state enterprises. This process was followed by a large reduction, about 5 per cent per year between 1974 and 1979, in the size of the social and economic sectors of the bureaucracy (Vegara, 1981).

Finally, the government launched a series of 'modernizations' or public policies aimed at replacing the old statist system by the new market model. These modernizations, as the former Minister of Labour José Piñera argued, set the basis for a 'silent revolution', changing the nature and role of the state, setting new parameters for the relations between the private and the public sectors, destroying organizations such as labour unions and reorienting future generations toward the new belief. Through these policies the government totally transformed the structure of rural property, the educational system, the organization and power of the municipalities, the labour laws, the laws that regulated the professional associations, and the social security and health systems.

Both the social security reform and the labour laws reforms were authored by José Piñera, a young economist who, although he had been trained at Harvard, was one of the stars of the Economic Team. Piñera's market philosophy was clearly reflected in the new labour laws and in the social security reform. In the area of labour relations he argued that:

> Collective negotiations should adjust themselves, but never replace the economic realities reflected in the labor market . . . the process of collective bargaining is not a mechanism through which the unionized workers are going to obtain salaries above those established by the market, securing income generated by another factor of production. (Piñera, 1979)

The total overhaul of the labour law system took place between 1979 and 1981 and aimed at creating a perfect labour market, eliminating collective bargaining, allowing massive dismissal of workers, increasing the daily working hours up to twelve hours, and eliminating the labour courts (DL 2200, Law 18018, DL 3648).

Piñera's views and those of other members of the Economic Team had a profound impact on the social security system.

The new social security and health policies

Since 1978, the social security and health systems have been thoroughly reformed. The central objective of the administration was not only to restructure the old system in order to eliminate some of its vicious practices, but most importantly to create a system attuned with the new economic model. In this section we will stress the new roles assumed by the state and the private sector, and the transformation of the social security system into a compulsory private insurance system, as well as the privatization of the administration of the funds.

Reform of the pension system

Just as previous governments have done in the past, the Pinochet regime attempted to reform the social security system very early in the administration, but in practice the government did not enact any major reforms until 1978 due to the political disputes that existed within the government regarding economic and social policies (Borzutzky, 1982).

In February of 1979 the administration enacted the DL 2448 which equalized benefits, eliminated pensions based on years of service, established a uniform system of pension readjustments, and eliminated the *perseguidoras*, which were special pensions received by high civil servants in which the size of the pension was equal to the current salary carried by the position occupied by the individual. There is no doubt that the decree addressed some of the most critical problems of the system such as inequities in the benefits and the problem of indexation, and eliminated two of its worst practices: the pensions based on years of service and the *perseguidoras*. What is important, also, is that these reforms had been attempted by President Frei and that he encountered an invincible opposition. Thus, what the democratic regime could not accomplish because of the power that civil servants had to obstruct any substantial reform, the authoritarian regime imposed with one stroke of the pen.

1980 was the year of the modernizations and José Piñera was charged with coordinating the labour and economic sectors of the government; institutionalizing a new system of labour relations, creating a free and depoliticized labour organization; and restructuring the social security system. According to Piñera the social security reform should involve the application of the principle of the subsidiary state regarding the administration and the financial structure of the system, should eliminate the portion of the social security tax paid by the employers in order to reduce the cost of labour and should maintain the principle of social solidarity only in relation to the minimum pensions (Larrain, 1981).

While the elimination of the wage tax was justified on the grounds that the tax distorted the labour market and limited the growth of employment, the need to transfer the administration of the system to private corporations was explained on the grounds that the provision of social security services was a function that could be performed either by public or private agents and that they could be best performed by the private sector since they required sophisticated financial techniques and a complex administrative system (Piñera, 1979). Accordingly, the reform involved: the creation of private corporations charged exclusively with the administration of social security funds (in order to ensure competition among them the law fostered the creation of multiple administrative entities); the elimination of the payroll tax paid by the employer, creating in practice a compulsory private insurance system financed with a 10 per cent contribution paid only by the insured; the creation of a system of minimum pensions based on the principle of solidarity. Piñera argued that a reform of this kind effectively contributed to reducing the relative size of the state and strengthening the private sector.

From a financial standpoint the reform introduced a number of essential modifications geared to reinforce individualism and to alter the principle of solidarity. The process of reduction of the employers' contribution had begun in 1975 and it ended with the 1980 law which eliminated the employers' portion of the wage tax paid to the pension fund, maintaining only a 1 per cent tax for the workman's compensation fund and a temporary 2.85 per cent tax to finance the family allowances and the unemployment insurance funds. Currently, the employer pays only 0.85 per cent to the workman's fund and 2 per cent into the unemployment fund. Employers' and workers' contributions were reduced substantially only for those workers who transferred their funds to the new system. The amount reduced changed from fund to fund.

Because of the emphasis on individualism, the 1980 reform replaced the common fund system by a system of individual capitalization. As Piñera argued, the new system 'established a clear relationship between personal effort and reward' and 'allows the individual to choose and decide about his or her future' (Piñera, 1980). The individual funds, in turn, were to be administered by private corporations created specially for this purpose, called *Administradoras de Fondos de Pensiones* (AFPs) or Pension Funds Managing Corporations. In order to secure a free market approach the law encouraged the creation of a plurality of private corporations. Their profits are derived from the commissions they charge for the administration of the funds. Finally, the new private funds were expected to have a positive impact on the private sector of the economy at large by contributing to the formation of a local capital market which, in turn, would foster economic development (Costabal, 1981).

Originally, twelve corporations were created and nine of them were owned by the largest economic groups that appeared in Chile as a result of the privatization policies pursued by the administration. The two largest corporations belonged to the two largest economic groups and they captured about 63 per cent of those insured in the new system. By the end of 1987 they still controlled about 50 per cent of the old pension funds (Mesa Lago, 1985).

In regard to benefits, the reform relies on the DL 2448 which had established a minimum retirement age of 65 years for males and 60 years for females, and a general requirement of at least ten years of contributions. The DL 3500, which contains the 1980 reform, and the modifications approved in 1987 established that once these basic requirements had been fulfilled the pensioner had three different options: first, to buy an immediate life annuity from an insurance company; second, to obtain a pension directly from a pension funds managing corporation; or third, to combine a temporary annuity paid by the fund with a deferred life annuity brought from an insurance company.

Finally, a system of minimum pensions was created which provides a pension in case of depletion of the individual account or if the rent produced by the fund is smaller than the minimum pension. In order to qualify for the pension the insured needs to have at least twenty years of contributions.

The new system was launched in May of 1981 and by the end of that year about 1.6 million people, more than half of the economically active population, had transferred their funds to a pension funds managing corporation. A major incentive for the workers to transfer to the new system was the large reduction in their portion of the tax, which ranged from 7.6 per cent for blue-collar workers to 17.1 per cent for bank employees. It is important to mention also that both the government and the pension funds managing corporations promoted the system through the most expensive publicity campaign in Chile's history. The campaign stressed the issues of modernity and self-reliance.

Two aspects of the new system are noteworthy: first, that it does not apply either to the military or to the police since they maintained their old funds and benefits; and second, that the reform involves the establishment of a state-enforced private insurance system since all new workers must join the new system and the old workers must remain in it if they decide to change.

Reforms in the health area

The central issue here has been also a redefinition of the role of the state following the principles of the subsidiary state. The administration rejected both a total commitment to the provision of health and total privatization. In practice, between 1974 and 1977 the health budget was constantly reduced and then it was reduced again in 1980 and 1981, falling behind its 1974 level (Mesa Lago, 1985). At the same time, there was an increase in the portion of the funds generated by the private sector which indicates the changing role of the state in this area (Scarpaci, 1988).

In 1979 the government reorganized the entire health system, replacing the National Health Service and SERMENA with the National System of Health Services which is charged with the provision of medical attention for both blue- and white-collar workers. The newly created system eliminated, then, the division along occupational lines and created a national system subdivided into regional units. Simultaneously, the government proceeded to consolidate the financial structure creating a common health fund, *Fondo Unico de Salud*, which is financed with contributions from the old pension funds, the state, and those enrolled in the pension funds managing corporations and who want to participate in this system.

In order to strengthen the role of the private health sector the government created the ISAPREs or *Institutos de Salud Previsional*, which provide an optional form of private health insurance modelled after Blue Cross and Blue Shield. Thus, in theory the insured can direct his or her contribution either to an ISAPRE or to the common health fund, but in practice the private health system is geared only to middle and upper income groups since the insurance companies are authorized to set a minimum income requirement for their subscribers. Enrolment in the ISAPREs reached about half a million and, just as in the case of the funds, the three largest ISAPREs control about 60–70 per cent of the market share.

Economic, social and political impact

As former Minister Piñera argued 'the social security reform has been one of the most important steps taken by the present regime. It constitutes a new and original scheme which will contribute decisively to change the economic and political culture of all Chileans' (Piñera, 1980).

The impact of this reform can be analyzed both from an economic and a sociopolitical perspective. From an economic standpoint the essential elements are the amount of the pension received by the insured and the impact of the reform on the economic performance of the country.

The pension received by the insured under the new system is a direct result of the deposits made by the individual plus the interest accrued, less the commissions charged by the pension funds managing corporation. The deposits, in turn, depend on the level of wages while the interest depends on the real rate of capital return. In regard to wages it is important to note that because of the nature of the economic policies pursued by the Pinochet regime, the real value of wages grew only 1.2 per cent between 1980 and 1988 while the real minimum wage declined by 28.5 per cent. During the same period, urban unemployment averaged 15.3 per cent per year. Clearly, both indicators should have a negative impact on the value of the pensions. Despite these indicators, the government estimated in 1987 that the value of a retirement pension paid by the new system was 1.24 times higher than one paid by the old system, while invalidity pensions appeared to be 2.23 times higher (Superintendencia de Administradoras de Fondos de Pensiones, 1987). The study was done on the basis of about 10,000 pensions already granted by the new system.

The structure of the commissions charged by the pension funds managing corporations also affects the value of the pension. As it stands now, after several reforms, the corporations charge a flat rate for the administration of the fund and this rate is by definition regressive.

From a larger perspective the reform was conceived as a mechanism geared to strengthen the private economic sector and to develop an indigenous capital market. Several processes need to be highlighted here. First is the fact that the capital accumulated by the new funds amount to about 13 per cent of GNP (Errázuriz, 1987). Second, that in order to protect those monies, investment of the funds had been closely regulated, but through the years these investment requirements have been liberalized allowing the private funds to invest in shareholding companies.

Another important element is the ownership of the new corporations. Their ownership was from the beginning tied to the 'economic groups', the large conglomerates that appeared as a result of the privatization policies of 1974–6. Thus, originally the largest corporations were owned by the two largest groups: the Vial and the Cruzat-Larrain groups. Following the 1982 recession two processes unfolded: first, these groups went bankrupt and their assets were temporarily administered by the state; second, the assets were re-privatized and at least part of them has been sold to foreign creditors since the administration has pursued a 'debt for equity scheme' according to which foreign creditors are encouraged to transform their credits in Chile into assets. As a result, a sizeable portion of these corporations is now totally or partially owned by US companies. Currently, the four largest funds are controlled by foreign corporations, including the US-owned Aetna and Bankers Trust and this certainly changes the impact that the funds have on the local economy.

From a social perspective the reform has substantially reduced the importance of the notion of solidarity, which is now applied only to the system of minimum pensions. Thus, in the new pension system the state intervenes at two different stages — at the outset, in order to enforce the enrolment in the new system, and at the end only by providing a very small pension to the lowest income groups.

Finally, what is important to stress from a political standpoint is the complementarity that existed between the authoritarian politics of General Pinochet and the principles of the monetarist approach, since both converged in their need to disarticulate powerful socio-political organizations that interfered with the hidden hand of the market. In this context, the social security reform was possible only because of the previous disarticulation of labour unions and professional associations and it contributed, in turn, to destroy the very strong pressure groups that had been created around the old pension funds. Moreover, because of the authoritarian nature of the regime the reforms were imposed upon the society by an authoritarian state. Thus, in spite of the fact that the reform was presented as allowing the individual to choose freely how to save for old age, in practice it is a compulsory system. As a former under-secretary of labour argued, 'the state has the obligation to protect the immature elements of the society who would not save for their old age unless they are forced to do so' (Mardones, 1981).

From a larger perspective what one sees, in the case of Chile and of other Latin American countries as well, is a very activist state. As James Malloy argued, 'the state has not been simply the passive object of group and class pressure, but an active constitutive force in its own right' (Malloy, 1979) and that a 'Technician Centred Decision-making style has characterized the policymaking process' both in the area of economic and social policies (Malloy, 1989). In the case of Chile, the state played a central role both in the processes of establishing the original social security system in 1924 and in the 1980 reform. What have changed are the goals of the state. Thus, while between 1924–73 the goals were geared by principles of political and economic inclusion of different socioeconomic groups, the goals after 1974 were defined in terms of the disarticulation and exclusion of political actors and the atomization of the society. The monetarist principles and the policies of the Chicago Boys provided the economic arguments and decisions required to achieve fully this task in the economic field, while the principles of the National Security Doctrine provided the political arguments.

Now, Chile has recuperated its democratic institutions, but the long-term impact of the policies of the radical right will be felt for a long time since the Aylwin administration is not planning any major overhaul of the economic structure. In the area of social policies the administration has only promised palliative measures such as increasing the minimum pensions and family allowances, and in general to pursue policies geared to increase the standard of living of the poorest sectors of the society. In practice, not even these minor steps have been taken yet.

What remains to be seen in Chile is the feasibility of this individualist approach to social security in the context of the new democratic environment and what kind of pressures will be placed on the state by labour unions, political parties and other social groups as they begin to compete openly in the political arena.

6

Social policy, the radical right and the German welfare state

Steen Mangen

The economic arguments of the radical right have been forcefully expressed in West Germany since the first oil crisis and, at least at the rhetorical level, have found an echo in pronouncements of Chancellor Kohl and other leading politicians in the Christian Democratic Union (or CDU) (conservatives) and among the Free Democrats (liberals). But how, if at all, has rhetoric been translated into practice in the formulation and subsequent implementation of social policy in the eight years of Kohl's premiership?

After a constructive parliamentary vote of no confidence in the then Social Democratic-led government, the Christian Democrat leader, Helmut Kohl, assumed the Chancellorship in 1982, promising to fulfil a broadly *New Right* agenda through his *Wendepolitik* (a policy of change): a neo-liberal economic strategy combined with a neo-conservative social policy which would eradicate the excesses of the *Vaterstaat*. He promised a deregulation of the German economy combined with a sustained effort to dismantle the effects of a distended and increasingly expensive welfare system that, moreover, stifled individual initiative.

The German welfare system, as with any other, is a specific cultural arrangement with innate constraints to which political reformers of left or right must respond if they are to be successful innovators. In this review of social security and family issues during the eight years of Kohl's Chancellorship, it will be argued that, in the event, radical right influence has largely been confined to the rhetoric of social policy. Neo-liberal reforms of social security have not been forthcoming, privatization of welfare provisions not having been seriously on the agenda, although there has been a search for a greater degree of commercialization and efficiency. On the other hand, there is clear evidence of conservative influence in the formulation of family policy. It could be argued that this merely reflects traditional Christian Democrat concerns rather than a significant *New Right* reconceptualization of the issue.

None the less, changing welfare objectives throughout the decade have seen the re-emergence of a 'classic' vocabulary of welfare to which has been added a new and fashionable lexicon. Considerable effort has been expended in exhorting the benison of 'self help', a welfare objective now espoused by other parties, albeit with differing interpretations. Similarly, the importance of the achievement and equivalence principles in social insurance have been reconfirmed, although with an ageing population the solidarity principle has been re-examined in an attempt to restore inter-generational equity. The issue of what Germans term the 'social symmetry' (broadly, fairness) of welfare retrenchments has also proved a challenge to the Chancellor. And, as elsewhere in Western Europe, the concept of marginalization gained currency, particularly through a CDU idea of a 'new social question' of groups in the population who have largely been excluded from the benefits of the welfare state. The issue of targeting and greater efficiency, thus, assumed a higher profile, but significantly 'citizenship', at least in terms of a basic social pension, was rejected by the coalition in favour of maintaining the transparency principle of the social insurance system. In Germany, perhaps more than elsewhere, the 1980s witnessed a gradual colonization by the major parties of the Greens' socio-ecology: the position that welfare gains should not be achieved at the cost of environmental damage.

Economic performance and social expenditure

The long-term high performance of the German economy is reflected in per capita GDP data which in 1988, in terms of purchasing power parities, was exceeded among EC states only by Luxembourg (see Table 6.1). After high growth in the pre-oil crisis period, performance in the 1980s has been less impressive and in 1981 and 1982 negative growth rates were recorded. As Table 6.1 indicates growth rates in the first five years of Kohl's tenure of the Chancellorship averaged

Table 6.1 The German social state in comparative perspective

	Germany	France	UK
A: Per capita GDP US$ 1988 purchasing power parities	13,323	12,803	12,340
B: GDP average annual volume growth, 1982–7	2.1	1.6	3.2
1987–8	3.4	3.2	4.2
C: Government social expenditure % GDP ... 1980	26.6	30.9	20.0
... 1986 (1)	25.2	34.2	20.6
of which education 1980	5.1	5.7	5.5
1986	4.5	6.1	5.1
health 1980	6.3	6.0	5.2
1986	6.3	6.7	5.3
pensions 1980	12.1	11.5	6.3
1986 (1)	11.4	12.5	6.6
unemployment 1980	0.9	1.6	1.0
1986 (1)	1.4	2.8	1.6
D: Total social protection expenditure, 1988 % GDP (2)	28.1	28.3	23.6
E: Social protection funding, 1987			
% Employer	41.1	52.2	27.9
% Employee	30.4	27.0	17.0
% Public Funds	25.2	18.2	43.4
% Other (3)	3.2	2.6	11.8
F: Social protection benefits per inhabitant in terms of purchasing power parities, 1987 ECU	4,603	4,279	3,452
G: Unemployment rate 1988 (4)	6.2	10.3	8.3
H: Long-term unemployment rate 1987	31.9	45.5	42.6

(1) French statistic is for 1985.
(2) UK statistic is for 1987.
(3) This category largely comprises receipts from interest on capital which in the case of the United Kingdom is derived from occupational pension funds.
(4) OECD standardized unemployment rates.

Sources: D, E, F: Rapid Reports: Population and Social Conditions, No. 3, Eurostat. Commission of the European Communities, 1990.
A, B, C, G, H: OECD in Figures. Supplement to OECD Observer, No. 158, Paris, OECD, 1989.

2.1 per cent and were below the EC average. However, current OECD estimates of GDP growth indicate a fairly respectable 2.75 per cent, although slower growth is expected in the 1990s, these estimates having been made before the implications of unification could be considered.

The performance of the German economy in the last decade demonstrates clearly the intransigent problem of unemployment. Even though the economic growth rate in 1988 was the highest for ten years, unemployment declined only slowly. Between 1983 and 1987 the rate averaged about 9 per cent and in 1988 had only fallen to 8.7 per cent. In the first quarter of 1990 the official rate amounted to 6 per cent of the economically active population. Critically, the proportion of the long-term unemployed has been rising to account for over 30 per cent of the total, although this is significantly below the rate for France and the United Kingdom (see Table 6.1). Typically, there are strong regional dimensions with the economically successful southern state of Baden-Wuerttemberg recording only a third of that in the northern city-state of Bremen.

Among the EC states, West Germany's social budget has been above average, in total consuming approximately one-third of GDP. Social budgets expanded rapidly during the 1960s and early 1970s, especially during the Brandt Chancellorship. Between 1969 and 1975, for example, social expenditure rose sharply in excess of economic growth rates from 24 to 33 per cent of GDP. Social security accounts for almost two-thirds of social expenditure, with health care consuming one-fifth and education much of the remainder. Significantly, the greater part of the social budget is financed through semi-autonomous social insurance schemes and by the federal states and local authorities.

Per capita welfare benefits, in terms of purchasing power parities in 1987, are 28 per cent above the EC average and are slightly exceeded only by the Netherlands and Luxembourg. Social insurance contributions account for almost 19 per cent of GNP and are among the highest in the OECD countries. In fact, social security budgets have been in surplus in the late 1980s, although this balance has been subsequently reduced by half because of improvements in benefits and increases in the number of pensioners. Federal subsidies to the insurance system have stabilized recently at about 12 per cent of total expenditure, much of this being allocated to the pension schemes.

Overall, during Kohl's premiership welfare allocations have been more tightly constrained by GDP performance than was the case for his predecessors. On Kohl's assumption of the Chancellorship, public social expenditure reached 25 per cent of GDP, but subsequently there was a reversal in trends, at least until the middle of the decade, although a part of this decline is attributable to policies initiated by Schmidt. In 1986, OECD data indicate that government expenditure was 1.4 percentage points less than in 1980. As Table 6.1 shows, ratio reductions were broadly shared by education and pensions. In the case of the former, the reduction is largely explained by the declining school-age cohort (the lowest in the EC) and by the replacement of student grants by loans. Pension allocations have suffered from reductions in entitlements by changes in indexation, for example, although significantly the data do not take account of the growing number of the elderly who are also partially dependent on social assistance. On the other hand, as a consequence of increasing unemployment, allocations there have inevitably increased. Current estimates of the total social budget project a further decline in GDP terms, from 31.1 per cent (1985) to 29.5 per cent (1990) because the higher economic growth rates achieved in the late 1980s have not been fully matched by increases in social expenditure. Significantly, this ratio will still exceed that attained in the early 1970s, before the first oil crisis (Kloss, 1990).

The German welfare system

Despite its permeation by Nazi officials and the suppression of direct elections for membership of the administrative boards, Hitler left the institutional arrangements of the social insurance system more or less intact. On German capitulation the Allies found a system that was functioning effectively and, moreover, a German institution that could still command international respect. Thus, despite pressures, both internal and external, to create a socialized system, an early decision was made to create a new German state that would retain its Bismarckian system of social insurance organized according to each contingency (sickness, old age and industrial accidents, to which unemployment was added in the 1920s).

In the German *Rechtstaat* a clear distinction is made between the welfare responsibilities of each tier of government — federal government, *Laender*, and communes and their status is guaranteed under the constitution. Furthermore, the subsidiarity principle enshrined in the constitution allocates to various 'citizen initiatives' a primary role for many welfare functions, the public sector in these cases being the provider of last resort. Voluntary agencies — the so-called 'free agencies' (*freie Traeger*) — administer many of West Germany's health and social services, and social insurance is organized on the self-administration principle by the social partners. It is, therefore, important to emphasize that the capacity of political leaders to push through their own policies in areas of shared responsibility is constitutionally restricted. For example, Thatcherite attempts to subdue local authorities by such strategies as 'rate-capping' would be impossible in Germany. A summary of responsibilities in this welfare 'complex' is given in Table 6.2.

Social insurance entitlements are closely regulated by the equivalence principle: that is, the benefits paid to those temporarily or

Table 6.2 The German welfare system

Federal government
- Oversees the social insurance system.
- Contributes to capital costs of services.
- Retains certain reserve functions: e.g., medical education, research in health and welfare, promotes 'model' services, regulates the 1961 Federal Social Assistance Act.
- Has an exhortative role: e.g., commissions enquiries, 'concerted federalism'.

Laender
- Have major responsibility for policy making and planning.
- Contributes to capital costs of services.
- Provides certain services: e.g., some hospitals.
- Largely fund 'last resort' means-tested social assistance.

Communes
- Undertake local policy making and planning of social services.
- Contribute to capital costs of services.
- Provide certain services: e.g., some hospitals and preventive health and welfare services.
- Administer and partly fund social assistance.

Voluntary sector
- The many separate agencies are organized into five *Spitzenverbaende*: two are denominational, one is allied to the trade union movement, one is the German Red Cross and the other an association of small agencies.
- Planning by these agencies is largely dictated by the availability of funding, with the result that there is no overall planning strategy.
- Contributes to capital costs of services.
- Each agency negotiates operating fees with the social insurance schemes and, where necessary, social assistance.
- Administers hospital services (37 per cent of all inpatient beds) and is the principal provider of a wide range of welfare services.

(continued on p. 106)

Table 6.2 — *continued*

Private sector

- Provides capital costs of services.
- Profit is dominant planning criterion.
- There are few restrictions on the establishment of services.
- Maintain some health and welfare provisions (e.g., 10 per cent of all hospital beds).
- Doctors in 'office' practice are the major providers of outpatient treatment receiving fees on an 'item of service' basis.

Social Insurance

- There are well over 1,000 sickness insurance funds: statutory schemes, 'replacement' schemes for white-collar workers and certain occupational schemes. They are variously organized at local, *Land* and federal level. They fund the operational costs of health services via a daily fee for each occupied bed and the treatment fees for each 'item of service'.
- 'Blue collar' pension schemes are administered by each *Land*. 'White collar' schemes are managed by a federal agency. There are certain separate occupational schemes. They provide old age, disability and survivors' pensions and fund the operational costs of rehabilitative services for the disabled.
- Social assistance is varyingly funded by each level of government. It provides means-tested cash benefits for those whose insurance entitlements have expired or are insufficient. In addition, it partly funds the operational costs of health and welfare services, especially for long-stay institutions, when liability is not accepted by the social insurance funds.
- The major funders negotiate fees separately with hospitals, medical associations and welfare agencies.
- Unemployment insurance is managed by a federal agency.
- There are various industrial accident schemes funded by employers.

Private individuals

- Liability for the costs of certain medical treatments and welfare facilities falls in part or whole on individuals and/or their families.
- Income of near relatives is taken into account in assessing social assistance.
- The community care policy identifies the family as the prime caring agency.

permanently out of the workforce should provide a broadly equivalent standard of living to that attained in former periods of employment. The relatively generous level of benefits, when compared internationally, has produced high electoral expectations which impose constraints on politicians' ability to implement reforms, as will be demonstrated later in the case of pensions. On the other hand, social assistance, which is funded and administered by local authorities is subjected to a harsher level of means-testing than was the case of British supplementary benefit, for example, and is generally regarded as attracting more stigma to recipients. The *Leistungsprinzip* — the objective of rewarding success in the labour market by high insurance benefits — has meant that redistributive goals have been secondary concerns, at least until recently. Indeed, the radical right has argued that social insurance must retain both its reward for economic achievement and the transparency of the system and that, where redistributive efforts are legitimate, they are more appropriately pursued through fiscal policy (Mangen, 1991).

The German social state and the politics of consensus

The constitutional arrangements of the Bonn republic were an explicit attempt to institute a meticulous system of checks and balances against possibilities of radical political reform. Consequently, the principal characteristic in the forty years since the 1949 constitution established the Federal Republic as a social state guaranteed under law (*sozialer Rechtstaat*) has been the achievement of a high degree of political and economic stability.

The influence of social catholicism is clearly at play in the establishment of the social state: the priority given to the subsidiarity of the state to other forms of political intermediation in order to avoid a repetition of dominant centralizing tendencies; the emphasis on conflict resolution through a reliance on the social partnership and self-administration of collective social provisions; the importance attached in economic and social policy making to corporatist arrangements and, in implementation, to 'concerted action' rather than centralized planning; the rejection of mass state ownership in favour of the free market, tempered by social guarantees through the operation of the 'social market economy'; and, importantly, the recourse of the individual to social and labour courts to protect welfare and occupational rights (Pilz, 1978).

Social catholic teaching was of particular importance in the early history of the Federal Republic and, indeed, the principles of Erhard's social market economy are a conscious attempt to construct a Christian Democratic state. Essentially, the Church attempted to regulate the relationship between the state, employers, employees, the family and the individual. Significantly, as Bosanquet (1983) has observed, the heritage of social catholicism has been an important counterweight to *New Right* attempts at renegotiation of state responsibilities. Originating in the search for an ultimate solution to the *Arbeiterfrage* and the implications of the growth of the secular state in the late nineteenth century, the Papacy exhorted the primacy of informal and private social arrangements over those of government. The seminal papal encyclical *Rerum Novarum* of 1891, portrayed the possibility of a more acceptable face for contemporary, brutal capitalism, by extending popular ownership, securing a fairer distribution of wealth, and guaranteeing extended suffrage and the rights of combination. The duties of the employer to the workforce were also reinforced by the promotion of existing empresarial welfare measures, particularly under the aegis of the catholic *patronat*. Subsequent encyclicals reiterate the Papacy's distrust of the secular state and, again, emphasize the principles of subsidiarity, solidarity and social integration (Krotz, 1988). Despite the insistence of *New Right* advocates in the 1970s and 1980s, it was never part of social catholic teaching to argue for the relegation of secular authorities to a marginal role, since the encyclicals attribute to the state the responsibility for supervising and fostering small-scale 'spontaneous' social arrangements (Richter, 1987).

The social market economy was Erhard's attempt to incorporate social catholic thought into a 'third way' which would eschew both *laissez-faire* and centralized planning as appropriate methods of economic management, while attention to a social dimension was intended to avoid a progressive stray into state welfarism (Barry, 1987). Respecting the Hegelian notion of the state as a neutral institution overseeing the negotiations of various groups in society from which it stands apart, the prime concern was to exclude the possibility of an overarching paternalist state by embracing a partnership or corporatist model. The economy was to be directed in a way that would instil widespread support for free enterprise through maintaining full employment, encouraging wide ownership of property and creating a viable regulatory system for capital accumulation. According to a by-now legendary dictum, for Erhard the 'best social policy is an effective economic policy'. But his understanding of the social dimension was a rejection of a robust redistributive role for the social state, since a strategic societal policy (*Gesellschaftspolitik*) as opposed to a narrower welfare policy (*Sozialpolitik*) would be more likely to support the generation of economic growth that would render redistribution superfluous.

Ultimately, the social element within the German model of the market is variously open to liberal or conservative interpretations which have never been satisfactorily reconciled. And, although all major parties were eventually to support the social market economy and have religiously reaffirmed their commitment to it in recent election manifestos, there has been a relaxation in governmental adherence since the Grand Coalition of the mid-1960s when overtures to Keynesian demand management were first made. Chancellor Kohl's stated intention, as part of his *Wendepolitik*, was to restore the model to its original state.

Since its inception, the republic has refined a strategy of cooperative federalism (Katzenstein, 1987) which endeavours to reconcile *Politikverflechtung*: the intermeshed responsibilities of different tiers of the political hierarchy. The federal states, the *Laender*, have major powers in social policy making and, through the powerful upper house of parliament, the *Bundesrat*, are able to maintain a strong influence on national policy for which, in any case, they are responsible for implementing (Bulmer, 1989). The federal government, therefore, has every incentive in maintaining a sound working relationship in order to secure the success of its policies. Furthermore, the regular round of *Laender* elections are an important influence in Bonn's relationship with the states and provide feedback on the governing parties' popularity which, as will be seen later, can encourage amendments to unpopular policies.

To a large degree, this cooperative tradition also extends to parliamentary processes where, in the specificities of policy formulation, there is considerable emphasis on the cross-party 'technical' nature (*Sachlichkeit*) of problems that requires consensus resolution (Vobruba, 1983). This inter-party negotiation arises from the nature of Germany's party system. The two main groupings: the Christian Democrats and the Social Democrats are *Volksparteien*, that is, electorally broadly based parties competing for the centre ground. The Christian Democrats and their Bavarian sister party, the CSU, integrate two traditions: social catholicism which is most clearly demonstrated in the SoPo (social policy) wing of the party and the neo-liberalism of the economic wing. SoPos acknowledge the supremacy of free enterprise but, in order to strengthen the image of a *Volkspartei*, they wish to retain a strong intermediary role for the state through minimum welfare guarantees and through regulation of the pluralist welfare system. The economic wing, on the other hand, argues for minimum state intervention and greater reliance on private provision. The duality of its electoral appeal requires sensitive management. For example, the trade union movement (DGB) has influential allies among SoPos and the CDU has always been at pains to avoid too close an identification as an unambiguously bourgeois party (Padgett, 1989). Thus, in comparative terms the post-war welfare record of the German Christian Democrats has been above the average for European conservative parties (von Beyme, 1985). And, in recent years, it has been particularly sensitive to the accusation of the SPD that it has created 'a two-thirds society' condemning one-third of the population to economic and social marginalization.

Crucially, the effects of the proportional representation (PR) voting system mean that, for all but a short period in the late 1950s, governments of either formation have had to form coalitions with the liberals (FDP) and, indeed, in the late 1960s the parties formed a Grand Coalition government. An adversarial tradition, at least at the point of policy enactment, is therefore largely absent. Apart from the early 1980s, at the time of the greatest retrenchment in social expenditure, broad cross-party compromise on important social policies has ultimately been negotiated. This is not to suggest that serious party political differences on social policy do not exist. Although overall positions on social security do not conform to a crude left–right distinction (Nissen, 1990), different positions were taken with regard to the creation of a minimum social pension, for example. Comprehensive education, too, has been a contentious subject. Roberts (1989) stresses that the political consensus is, rather, more to do with policy-making procedures than initial policy proposals. As will be seen later in the case of pensions, the parties may begin the negotiating process from very different stances but during the formulation phase have been willing to compromise on specific elements in the interests of securing a broadly acceptable policy package.

The German style of policy making is not without negative consequences. Inter-party manoeuvres can stifle effective consideration of policy alternatives because of the often relatively narrow 'technical' understanding of social issues. Only in the 1980s did the fledgling political movement, the Greens, begin to force open a wider debate about welfare problems. The overriding requirement to generate and sustain a broad level of consensus at various points in the political system, as Heinze and Hinrichs (1986) argue, means that many radical and innovative policy alternatives have to be discarded because of their low feasibility in the face of conflicting vested interests manifest in the complex network of negotiations.

The *Wendepolitik*

Increasing disenchantment of the FDP, with Schmidt's response to the second oil crisis, combined with negative growth in the early 1980s, exacerbated relationships within the SPD–FDP coalition. Kohl's exhortation of the need for radical economic and social reform — his *Wendepolitik* — was, in part, a tactic to court the FDP, then dominated by their neo-liberal economic wing. In the event, the Liberals were unable to force their SPD cabinet partners to impose even tighter budgetary control and a parliamentary vote of no confidence resulted in the formation of a coalition government of the Union parties and the FDP under the chancellorship of Kohl.

In his first government declaration the Chancellor stressed the urgent need for social sacrifices. He indicted ever-rising welfare expenditure as one of the principal causes of the swift downturn in the German economy. A profound change of direction constraining the overgrown welfare state — a *Wendepolitik* — would, he insisted, have a positive outcome by bringing to the fore a debureaucratized, decentralized, small-scale and community-centred system. It would ensure more freedom, choice and self-realization by enabling individuals and their families to help themselves towards a greater degree of independence.

Inevitably, under Kohl the CDU SoPos lost ground, although tactically the Ministry of Labour was allocated to a leading member of their group. On the other hand, the influence of the FDP increased throughout the decade. This bourgeois party, whose principal constituency is the business community and self-employed professionals, increased pressure on the Chancellor for a radical liberalization of the economy and an overhaul of the welfare system through the infusion of greater competition by extending its pluralist character (for instance, by ending the monopoly of the federal unemployment scheme) and by promoting private provision (for instance, by introducing incentives for private pensions).

The central tenet of Kohl's policy was to argue for a 'new' subsidiarity of the state through the promotion of self help, more efficient use of public resources, privatization of part of the public sector, deregulation of the economy and more flexibility in the labour market and in allied social security regulations. In social policy the extolling of self help at times reached farcical proportions, the CDU *Ministerpresident* of Lower Saxony promising personally to serve free coffee (surely a contradiction!) to those who, by dint of their own efforts, reduced their dependence on social assistance. Privatization and commercialization of social services were important objectives, as was a conscious attempt to moderate welfare demand through consumer contributions to costs. The renewed emphasis on private provision also extended to housing policy. Relaxation of legislation on private building for rent was promised, as was an improvement in the rights of the landlord *vis-à-vis* the tenant. The Chancellor also announced his intention to phase out allocations for social housing construction and to concentrate effort in this sector on building for owner occupation. Flexibility of the labour market was also a key goal, with more emphasis on job creation through part-time and short-term contracts and a relaxation of redundancy arrangements.

Fiscal reform was a central feature of Kohl's strategy. The policy was concretized by the introduction in the mid-1980s of the largest tax reform since the Second World War, to be implemented over four years. By comparison with Britain, reductions were modest and, in total, accounted for less than 2.5 per cent of GNP. Among other changes, the top marginal rate of income tax was reduced from 56 to 53 per cent (OECD, 1989). Public expenditure reductions were also announced under which the GDP take would be reduced by 1995 from the prevailing 46 per cent to 39 per cent and future public expenditure projections were to be held firmly in line with GDP growth. Budgetary retrenchment measures have also featured prominently and were at their most intense in the first three years of Kohl's period in office. In those years over 250 measures were implemented which had deleterious welfare effects (Baecker and Naegele, 1986). To be sure, the repertoire of cuts were similar to those taken by governments of left and right elsewhere in Europe: reductions in health, pensions, unemployment and family benefit entitlements, for example, were achieved by measures widely adopted in other countries. However, the mid-1980s electorally was a bad time for the Chancellor, with a series of defeats in *Laender* elections. These, combined with an upturn in the economy, encouraged the government to make some concessions on social entitlements, particularly for the older unemployed and by extending child allowances to the young unemployed. As will be discussed later, there was increased activity in the area of family policy. However, these welfare advances only partially reinstated earlier welfare losses (Grottian, 1988). The disappointing election result in 1987 (although the CDU continued as the senior party in the government) has provoked a renewed effort in welfare, particularly in pensions reform, where, as will be seen, a partial fiscalization of the system, rather than *ad hoc* federal subsidies, has now been institutionalized (Mangen, 1989).

Substantive policy reforms under Kohl

Health policy

Any radical reform of the German health system has been seriously constrained historically by the strong bargaining position of suppliers in the policy-making process aided by their political ally, the FDP (Zapf, 1986). On the other hand, Murswieck (1985) argues that the funders — the sickness insurance schemes — have been unable to gain much influence over the quality, quantity or distribution of the services supplied. Political energy in the 1980s has been devoted to finding means of reducing costs in a liberal health system where outpatient treatment is reimbursed on an item-of-service basis and the inpatient sector attracts a daily fee for each occupied bed, both of which manifest perverse incentives to oversupply. Effective cross-sector planning capacities have also been restricted by the pluralist nature of the system. Characteristically, German governments have relied on corporatist 'concerted actions' to contain expenditure which have largely been formulated and monitored by health suppliers. There have also been a range of cost control measures which have limited entitlements to certain treatments and have increased patient contributions. However, since the mid-1980s the Federal Government has been making a determined effort to increase its overall control of funding while surrendering some of its direct expenditure responsibilities. In 1984 the joint funding of hospital construction was superseded by measures which transferred competence to the *Laender*. Legislation in 1986 sought to stabilize inpatient costs by means of a prospective annual hospital budget which is calculated on expenditure patterns in the previous year. There are financial incentives to reduce lengths-of-stay which are long by international standards and increase the bed turnover rate. Correspondingly, there are penalties for hospitals where bed activity rates are lower than projected. Altenstetter (1986) cautions against too positive an interpretation of this measure. In an empirical study of its impact she argues that the new policy essentially leaves the sickness insurance system intact in terms of its total liabilities and is better understood as a consolidation of former 'concerted action' programmes.

The most important reform of health care was announced in 1987. Government advisers and the *Bundesbank* had urged a more market-orientated reform. But pressure from the SoPo wing of the CDU, including the minister responsible for its implementation, meant that radical structural change was not on the agenda and, instead, a carefully constructed package was put forward that retained the essential features of the system while appearing to offer something new to everyone. The package, which was enacted in 1989, increased patient contributions, further restricted 'luxury' treatments such as spa cures and sanctioned a limited pharmaceutical list for prescription reimbursement. It also proposed to extend the 'no claims' bonus that private sickness funds already offered. Significantly, of the projected 14 billion marks to be saved, half will go towards a 1 per cent reduction in insurance levies. The rest will be used by the sickness schemes to fund a new programme of long-term community care for the elderly in need of intensive home nursing and for the severely disabled. Informal carers are offered tax incentives, an attendants' allowance and four weeks holiday relief a year with a guarantee of a replacement carer, supplemented from 1991 by up to twenty-five hours a month of professional support. A further expansion of locally-based 'social wards' — local centres coordinating outpatient and day care facilities and domiciliary services such as meals on wheels — was intended to provide many of the benefits in kind (Luetke, 1988).

In fact, there had been discussion among the major parties in the mid-1980s of the potential for a supplementary care insurance, either integrated into the existing sickness and pension schemes or organized independently. In the face of opposition from the sickness funds the government eventually discarded the idea because it feared its existence could stimulate higher demand for institutional care in old age. The inclusion of the community care element in the health reform was, in part, an attempt to offer some innovative element to critics within the Union parties and Opposition who complained of the disappointing nature of the total package. The government made clear that it was only prepared to allocate to the community care programme the amount saved elsewhere in the health system: in other words, there was no new money involved. Yet, the sickness funds expressed their doubt that all the projected savings would accrue in reality and that, once in operation, they and the government would be unable to resist demands for further funding. Since the passing of this package the 'crisis of care' (*Pflegenotstand*) has once again become a priority slogan on the agenda of social issues facing the government and it has conceded that the 1987 reforms cannot be construed as a long-term solution. Currently, the SPD are proposing an extension of sickness fund liabilities supplemented by federal subsidies. The FDP wish to encourage private care. CDU SoPos also support a subsidized — or what is called a 'solidarity' — solution, but the labour minister is at present insistent that proposals that incur an extended role for the sickness funds have little feasibility (Noeldeke, 1990).

Opponents of the reform argue that the government unwisely shirked the necessary restructuring of the health care funding and delivery system, particularly in view of the ageing population and its consequences for future medical demands. Instead, they argue, the reform is merely a cost-cutting exercise that transfers the burden to patients and their families, views which contemporary surveys indicated were shared by a majority of the electorate and which, in fact, were demonstrated by the relatively poor showing of the CDU in the 1987 election. There is concern that increased economic, social and psychological costs will accrue to home carers, despite the improved benefits for which, in any case, there are strict entitlement criteria. The labour minister responded to accusations about a lack of social symmetry in these reforms by pointing out that suppliers — particularly the medical profession and the pharmaceutical industry — had to accept their share of cuts too. However, the pharmaceutical companies occupy a powerful position in the health negotiation process and threatened court action against the idea of state-imposed prices for their products, for which they obtained the support of FDP politicians. In the event, they appear to have won the day and the price reduction plans have been dropped (Alber, 1991).

The 1987 reforms veered away from reform of the sickness insurance system, although there have been some piecemeal changes in the direction of empowering the schemes to impose greater cost control. From 1989 sickness fund expenditure may not exceed growth in earnings. The government has also encouraged the schemes and the *Laender* to terminate contracts with expensive and superfluous hospitals. Overcapacity is a serious problem in Germany: official statistics estimate that there are currently 85,000 surplus beds. There are doubts, however, that the new policy will have much of an impact, given that primary responsibilities lie with the *Laender* who, in the interests of local economies, may be unwilling to be seen to be adopting unpopular measures such as closing hospitals. It is expected that, in the aftermath of their election victory in 1990, the Union parties will put forward proposals for structural reform of the insurance funds, which number well over one thousand. This is now all the more urgent, given the incorporation of the former East German health system into that of the West German. The principal concern is to increase the 'solidarity' aspect by finding acceptable mechanisms for cross-subsidization of the schemes. The aim is to reduce the mounting burdens of the local general schemes which, unlike the complementary 'replacement' schemes whose members are principally white-collar workers, have to accept all applicants and therefore bear the heaviest demographic and medical risks.

Pensions policy

Prior to unification West Germany was faced with the prospect that in 2030, because of a sharp decline in the proportion of workers to pensioners, pension fund contributions would have to double if current entitlements were to be maintained. Clearly, such a rate would impose heavy costs on industry with obvious implications for international competitiveness. The government has been attempting to educate today's workers to expect less from tomorrow's pension system. One of the major pensions issues, then, concerns the potential breakdown of the 'generational contract'. Another concerns the inequalities in pensions provision. Because they are earnings-related, variations in pension entitlements are considerable. Women, especially, have been adversely affected and their pensions profile is considerably inferior to that of men, irrespective of occupational group. In addition, the cut in the real value of pensions during the 1980s has seen increasing numbers of the elderly relying on top-up social assistance payments from local authorities.

Since the mid-1980s the SPD, the Greens and SoPo elements within the CDU have called for the establishment of some form of national minimum pension funded by general taxation. The SPD also proposed that pensions should henceforth be funded by a tax on turnover rather than by contributions for each worker which it argued depressed employment opportunities. For their part, the Greens favoured a 'machine tax' in part to compensate for environmental damage caused by technological innovations. Conversely, the FDP proposed an expansion of the pluralist pensions system by encouraging voluntary private pensions (at present accounting for less than 10 per cent of expenditure) within a tripartite system that, in addition, would comprise an insurance-funded minimum pension and complementary occupational schemes.

The SPD collaborated in a '*grosse Koalition der Vernunft*' with the other parties in the parliamentary task of reformulating the specificities of a new pensions model and in arriving at a new pensions formula. The result was a classic German political compromise. For example, the government had wanted a rapid reinstatement of 65 as the pension age, but the SPD managed to obtain a slower implementation. On the other hand, the Social Democrats had to sacrifice their machine tax proposal and the idea of a basic social pension, although future calculations for pensions incorporate a notional minimum income. Private pension solutions were not adopted but the privileged position of the non-contributory civil service pension was more or less retained. Significantly, the government accepted a partial fiscalization of the pension system in order to increase the 'solidarity' dimension and stabilize funding. Also part of a solidarity objective was the adoption of indexation on changes in net rather than gross earnings by which current pensioners will share in the burden of increases in the total deductions from current salaries. The possibilities of early and partial retirement were retained but incentives to extend working life were reinforced.

The pensions reform has predictably retained most of the existing features of the system. Although, clearly an attempt to stabilize the system, the policy has been regarded by critics as a short-term solution that represents the soft option and transfers the burden onto future generations of Germans. Be that as it may, the package does contain innovations, specific reforms being intended to serve wider policy objectives in family and health care. For example, the 'baby years' formula, first introduced in 1986, by which elderly women (or their male survivors) were attributed pension contributions for each child they had had, was extended from one to three years' credits, a measure first proposed by the Greens. Family and friends caring for the elderly or severely disabled at home are also credited with pension contributions for periods they provide support. In both cases, the government was attempting to resolve long-term problems: it hoped the 'baby years' would lead to an increase in the birth rate, thus providing a larger workforce to pay for pensions in the next century; and it was argued that credits for carers would diminish their call on social assistance, thereby reducing the financial burdens of the *Laender* and local authorities, and limit demand for expensive institutional care.

Women and family policy

It is in the area of family policy that what could be termed *New Right* influence has been most apparent, although it could be argued that in many ways the traditional Christian Democrat preoccupation with the sanctity of the family has merely been continued. However, Kohl has eschewed a specific pro-natalist policy, given its association with policies pursued in the Third Reich, and has adopted measures which it is hoped will indirectly improve a birth rate that, with Italy, is the lowest in the EC and has been declining rapidly, at least until the late 1980s. Women have been a prime target of the *Wendepolitik* both in their roles as mothers and carers. Faced with falling female electoral support for his party, the Chancellor was astute enough ostentatiously to add women's affairs to the family minister's portfolio, albeit without conferring on her significant additional powers. None the less, the women's section of his party walked out during his speech at a recent CDU national conference in protest at what they perceived as inaction on his part. The Chancellor's neo-conservative views on the family have been reflected most in policy output since the mid-1980s, in measures which partially reversed his earlier cuts in family expenditure. A child-rearing allowance (*Erziehungsgeld*), in addition to existing child benefit, was introduced in 1986 and maternity leave arrangements were improved. In the same year the 'baby credit' of pensions contributions was announced.

The child-rearing allowance was clearly intended to encourage working mothers to remain at home to look after their infants. Tax policy in favour of couples with one non-working partner also reinforced this goal. The allowance is payable immediately after maternity leave ends and initially lasted for one year, although this was subsequently increased to eighteen months. For the first six months there is a flat-rate benefit (600 DM) which can be paid either to women or to men, though to date all but a small percentage have been women. Thereafter, the allowance is means-tested for one year. Although a welcome addition to the more prosperous working couple, the flat-rate benefit has been criticized for discriminating against poor families — and especially single mothers — who would be unlikely to be able to give up work and subsist on the allowance. There have also been reservations about the inflexibility of the regulations permitting part-time work.

Neo-conservative views are at their most unambiguous in relation to abortion. Germany has comparatively strict rules, and pressures to liberalize the legislation of the mid-1970s, which reached the statute book only after an embittered battle, have been resolutely repelled. The CDU remains at heart a Catholic party and even proposals by the then SoPo minister for health, family and youth affairs, Rita Suessmuth, herself a liberal catholic, for a 'third way' solution to the problem through improved consultation procedures was strongly opposed within her own party, including by the Chancellor. Indeed, one product of the Christian Democratic position has been the establishment in 1986 of the 'Mother and Child Foundation', one of its principal aims being to provide monetary assistance to women considering abortion on social grounds, which critics have dismissed as compensation by benevolent assistance for the forfeiting of social rights.

The German labour market remains one of the most gender unfriendly in Europe, despite the projected need (at least until unification) for additional sources of labour. Women comprise only 39 per cent of the labour force, a rate which is significantly below the OECD average and they are heavily concentrated in fifteen typical 'female' occupations. Moreover, the German welfare system has not offered women the alternative employment avenues that has been the case in other countries (Esping-Andersen, 1990). The short school day and the rigidity of shop opening hours combine to make life difficult for the working woman. Traditionalist elements within the Union parties remain actively hostile to the modest measures Kohl has sanctioned to increase the female participation rate, which include proposals for a small expansion of crèche facilities. There have been federal schemes aimed at integrating or reintegrating women into the labour market, but a proposal by Suessmuth for female quotas in public sector management met with a cool response in cabinet. Legislation in 1985 reformed part-time employment conditions but Pfarr (1988) argues that this merely strengthened the employer's position, since most of the expansion in this sector has been in employment incurring too few weekly working hours to qualify for social insurance coverage and other labour market entitlements.

In evaluating the CDU's position on women, Haug (1986) asserts that in the 1980s the party actively promoted the myth of motherhood as a smokescreen for reprivatizing women's issues through promoting community care and care of children. But Chamberlayne (1991) stresses that, within the CDU, there are different emphases in family policy. She identifies a change of direction in the mid-1980s period away from sentimentalized views of the family unit and the existence of 'new motherhood' based on equality of status between housewives and working women to more active 'flexible' labour market policies, especially by promoting part-time employment, and exhortations of gender sharing of domestic tasks. For Chamberlayne the new orientation is 'cleverly ambiguous' because it retains many elements of the traditional role of women while appearing to promote career opportunities, but is ultimately pandering to the needs of the dual labour market.

The *Wendepolitik*: an assessment

Kohl belongs to that select company of political leaders of the left and right who came to power in the late 1970s or early 1980s claiming to have radical solutions for the deepening economic crisis: Reagan, Thatcher, Mitterrand and Gonzalez. All held office for a sufficient period to implement their vision of the future. Yet Kohl is perhaps best compared with Gonzalez, for neither made any serious or consistent attempt to enact more than piecemeal elements of the broad programme envisaged. Kohl was no political theorist or a man passionately advancing a new post-collectivist concept integrating the various positions held on the right. At heart, the Chancellor was a party manager, a tactician whose primary concern was to balance interests in what became an increasingly fractious coalition.

Thus, the *Wendepolitik* rarely ventured beyond the rhetoric of a 'historical new beginning'. To be sure, there is some substance to the argument that an attempt was made to stimulate self and mutual help through, for example, his community care policy. Yet, it represented a marginal innovation in relation to the dimension of the problem of long-term care confronting Germany. Shortly after its enactment it was generally acknowledged that a more comprehensive solution was urgently required. And, if privatization was an important objective of the Chancellor, he signally missed opportunities to promote his goals in the health and pensions reforms that were legislated. Policy was largely confined to changes in entitlements rather than with innovation of institutional arrangements. Private sector solutions for pensions which had been supported by the FDP were regarded as too insecure a basis for a new system, given the demographic projections and economic volatility. Indeed, rather than incorporating a private dimension, the Chancellor sanctioned a partial fiscalization of funding. On the other hand, a 'citizenship' solution, through the establishment of a flat-rate minimum social pension, was rejected in favour of strictly maintaining the equivalence principle. In a recent report, the OECD (1989) judge that these relatively modest changes will make further social security reform inevitable, an assessment which is surely reinforced by the added effect of unification. Elsewhere in the public sector, privatization has occurred on a very modest scale. Some local authorities have privatized cleansing services and there has been a growing reliance on private long-term nursing facilities, although this has been an *ad hoc* rather than planned development. A wider privatization programme failed to materialize in the face of the opposition from many CDU-led *Laender* who viewed it as a divestment in regional aid. Nor was there a call for people's capitalism through wider share ownership (Esser, 1988). That other *leitmotiv* of the *Wendepolitik*, the family, has also been the object of innovation but, again, it could be argued that, in essence, the new policies are largely a continuation of past CDU concerns in this area and the expenditure allocated only partially restores earlier cuts.

Cost containment remained a principal objective but, in many ways, measures were a continuation of Schmidt's *ad hoc* policies and in the mini-boom of the mid-1980s they were relaxed as a result of poor electoral performance in the *Laender* and the looming general election in 1987. 'Consolidation' of the budget, rather than a dismantling of the welfare system consistently remained the primary concern and, from the beginning, Kohl's social policies have never risen above a *Sparpolitik*. Initially, the cuts were *ad hoc* and short term but since the mid-1980s there have been attempts in health and pensions to arrive at long-term stability of expenditure. By the mid-1980s only half the volume of budgetary retrenchment initially announced had been realized (Alber, 1988). The impact of retrenchment measures was felt more harshly by some clientele than others, producing allegations of a lack of social symmetry on the part of the opposition for which the CDU paid the price in the 1987 election, which although it retained power, produced the party's worst result in the history of the republic. According to OECD data, government social protection expenditure between 1980 and 1986 declined in GDP ratio terms by almost 1.5 percentage points, although in part this was a product of the actions taken by the previous government. Education and pensions more or less equally explain the decline in expenditure ratios. The effects of the declining birth rate account for most of the former. And, although there were reductions in the quality of entitlements, pensioners in the 1980s suffered rather less than other social security recipients from the cuts in terms of the purchasing power of their benefits (Alber, 1988).

One of the achievements of the *Wendepolitik* lay in the public's capacity to expect less, a lesson they had begun to learn under Schmidt. Surveys in the early 1980s indicated that a majority of respondents favoured cuts in social security to increases in taxation. And, indeed, the Chancellor has managed to be elected three times, albeit with varying majorities. Significantly, the *Wendepolitik* succeeded in discrediting the expansion of the welfare system from the late 1960s as having been a SPD excess for which the price was now having to be paid. At the federal level the SPD has been struggling with its identity for the best part of a decade. The party has been forced to respond to the rhetoric of the *Wendepolitik* by acknowledging that welfare expenditure needs to be more closely tied to economic performance and that there needs to be greater efficiency in the use of welfare resources and more flexibility in labour market regulations. None the less (although admittedly largely for other reasons), the Social Democrats obtained their worst result since 1959 in the general election of 1990.

It should be apparent by now that, at root, it is the nature of the German polity that renders single-minded *New Right* social reform impossible. Even if the Chancellor was seriously convinced by his own rhetoric, he was too astute a politician to ignore the constraints of coalition government, consensus management, the demands of cooperative federalism and the image of the CDU as a *Volkspartei*. In the formulation of social policy he continued to rely on pre-existing processes of corporatist decision making involving the social partners, the *Laender*, the social insurance funds, the plurality of voluntary organizations and the private sector. There are, in any case, important constitutional guarantees against a radical dismantling of the welfare system. The social and labour courts have played an important role not only in adjudicating on cuts in entitlements in individual cases but also, as a result, in determining the policy line the government thinks is feasible. In this regard, too, there has been no Thatcherite onslaught on trade unions. While there have been some limitations on the right to strike and a relaxation of redundancy rules, for example, the unions have continued to enjoy the status of social partner in policy making rather than the position of discredited outcasts they had in the Britain of the 1980s (Koelble, 1988).

In the United States and the United Kingdom radical right politicians gained the ascendancy after electoral disenchantment with the record of the outgoing government. This was less the case in Germany. Over the long run it had experienced the classic economic miracle and contemporary economic problems, admittedly serious, had been of comparatively short duration. There had been no long decline in the German economy and its welfare system enjoyed popular esteem. There were no winters of discontent or lengthy waiting lists for hospital treatment. It could therefore be argued that bold and radical reforms were too politically risky and did not, in any case, assume the urgency they did elsewhere.

The personality of the political leader has been an important factor in successful implementation of radical right-wing thought. Kohl has never been strong on public image and it is easy to portray him as a dull, lacklustre 'backroom' politician. Fundamentally, the Chancellor is a conservative catholic who has preferred the role of managing the differing viewpoints within his cabinets to pushing through his own policies, although some have reservations about his success in this regard. At heart, Kohl lacks the strength of personality of politicians like Thatcher and Reagan, and as Smith (1989) rightly points out, he has never attempted to continue the assertive 'Chancellor democracy' that prevailed under Schmidt.

7

The radical right and social welfare in Israel

Howard Jacob Karger and Menachem Monnickendam

Israel has long been recognized as the only country in the Middle East with a true Western-style democratic social welfare state. With an extensive social security programme, comprehensive health care, a system of public housing, commodity subsidization and free education, Israel has allowed the majority of its Jewish citizens to achieve a high standard of living despite relatively low wages. This chapter will examine the history, structure and provisions of the Israeli social welfare state. Second, the chapter will investigate the complex relationship between the Israeli right and the welfare state. Third, the chapter evaluates the impact of the radical right on the ideas, policies and programmes of the Israeli welfare state.

Israel: the current realities

In many ways, Israel is a phenomenon in the Middle East. Small by international standards, Israel has a total land area of 21,500 square kilometres (excluding the West Bank and Gaza but including the Golan Heights), and a total population of about 4.3 million. Of that population, 13.8 per cent are Muslim, 2.3 per cent Christian and 1.7 per cent Druse and other. Although the percentage of children as part of the Israeli population is dropping, it is higher than in any OECD country (only Ireland approaches it). Conversely, the proportion of elderly is lower in Israel than in OECD countries (Kop, 1988). Over

75 per cent of Israelis live in urban areas (Central Bureau of Statistics, 1987).

The Israeli population is well educated. The median years of study for men is 11.4 years and for women 10.9 years. Of the OECD countries, only the United States (12.6 years) and Canada (11.8 years) have higher levels of education than Israel's for men; and only the United Kingdom slightly outperforms Israel with respect to women (11.0 years) (Kop, 1988).

In general, health indicators for Israel reflect an erratic system of health care. An Israeli male in the 1980s can expect to live an average of 72.5 years. This mortality rate puts Israel on almost the same level as Norway, Sweden, Switzerland and the Netherlands. On the other hand, life expectancy for females (76.2 years) is less impressive, and Israeli women live two years less than the average for OECD countries. While in 1960 there were 27 infant deaths (i.e., before age one) per 1,000 live births in the Jewish population, by 1985 that figure declined by 63 per cent to less than 10 infant deaths per 1,000 live births. On the other hand, the infant mortality rate among the non-Jewish population is almost twice as high — 18 deaths per 1,000 live births — a figure almost proportional to the white and black infant mortality rate in the United States. Although Israel's infant mortality rate is 40 per cent higher than OECD countries and is surpassed only by Greece, its perinatal mortality (death occurring late in pregnancy or in the first week of birth) rate is lower than the United States, Great Britain and France (Kop, 1988).

Although Israel traditionally had a low unemployment rate (employment policy was a priority for the Labour government that ruled Israel from 1948 to 1977), by mid-1990 it rose to over 9 per cent and thus approximated the unemployment rate of many Western European nations. The current recession that began in 1985, plus the residual impact of the savage inflation of the mid-1980s, has led to serious economic problems for Israeli workers. The average annual wage for the 18–24 age group was 63 per cent of the national average in 1970; by 1984 it fell to 47 per cent. Relative wages for the entire 18–44 age group declined between 1970 and 1984 (Kop, 1988).

While housing has improved over the past twenty-five years, Israel suffers from serious overcrowding compared to Western European nations. The Israeli average of 1.3 persons per room is double that of most OECD countries and 45 per cent higher than Ireland, the OECD country with the highest housing density. While two-thirds of households in OECD countries have relatively low housing density (less than one person per room), that spaciousness is enjoyed by only 33 per cent of Israeli households. Over 18 per cent of Israelis (compared with 3 per cent in OECD countries) live in severely overcrowded housing (i.e., two or more persons per room). On the other hand, Israel outperforms all OECD countries with respect to the availability of baths, showers and toilet facilities in domestic dwellings; only 3 per cent of Israeli households lack a bath or shower and only 1 per cent lack a toilet (Kop, 1988).

Israel's 14.5 per cent poverty rate (the poverty threshold is based on persons living below 50 per cent of the median income per standard adult) is similar to the United States, but significantly higher than many Western European nations. Moreover, income inequality is greater in Israel than in the United States and other OECD nations, with the exception of West Germany (Kop, 1988). The richest 10 per cent in Israel has 7.6 times more disposable income than the poorest decile. The top 1 per cent earned 17.7 per cent of the total disposable income in the economy, while the bottom tenth received only 4.4 per cent (*The Israeli Economist*, 1989a).

The modern history of Israel is marked by war and struggle. For most of its forty-one year history, Israel has either been at war or in preparation for one. In the pre-state period of the 1930s and 1940s, Israel was involved in armed struggle to force the British from Palestine. When the British mandate ended in 1948, Israel immediately found itself in a life and death struggle against a concerted attack from five Arab armies. The human cost of Israel's War for Independence was immense. Out of the 600,000 Jews living in Palestine in 1948, over 1 per cent or 6,000 were killed. On a proportionate basis, the Israeli fatalities were higher than the total casualties experienced by Americans in the two major world wars (Collins and Lapierre, 1982).

Apart from the War of Independence, the most decisive war occurred on 6 June 1967 when Israel defeated the armies of Egypt, Jordan and Syria, and thus enlarged its governed territory threefold. The Six Day War was followed by a surprise attack from Egypt and Syria on the Jewish high holy day of Yom Kippur in 1973. Despite early military setbacks, Israel was able to hold onto its governed territories. The last war — The Peace for Galilee Campaign (the War in Lebanon) — occurred in 1982 when Israel invaded Lebanon after repeated terrorist attacks on border villages in northern Israel. These wars, plus the need to constantly maintain an alert and modern military, has contributed to a very costly public sector.

While the economic level in Israel — at least as measured by income and GDP — is below many of its Western European neighbours, it is nevertheless an advanced industrial nation. (Because Israel has a large 'grey economy' — a non-taxed black market for employment and goods — it is difficult to accurately calculate wages and GNP. Some economists estimate that Israel's 'grey economy' equals one-third of total GNP.) For example, the Human Development Index of the United Nations Development Programme ranks Israel twentieth, just slightly below the United States and Austria (*The Economist*, 1990a). However, as with most modern industrial countries in the 1990s, Israel is plagued with income inequality, high unemployment and myriad social problems.

The development of social services in pre-state Israel

The ideological orientation of Israel as a Jewish state is based on Zionism: the creation of a just society rooted in egalitarian principles (Doron, 1976). The 40,000 (mostly secular) Jews who escaped from the pogroms of Eastern Europe to come to Palestine at the beginning of the twentieth century, found other Jews living in holy cities like Jerusalem, Tiberias and Safed. These Jews were religious, and to a large extent maintained by the financial support of their brethren in the diaspora.

The values of these religious Jews were rooted in capitalism and charity; ideas that were abhorrent to the Zionist pioneers (Medding, 1972). For the socialist Zionists it was a matter of principle that only those who lived by their labour (and did not exploit the work of others) were entitled to be legitimate members of the new community. Work became the central focus for people's civic rights (Schindler, 1980).

Life in pre-state Palestine was hard. Apart from coping with an antagonistic Arab population, the pioneers were faced with malaria, cholera, trachoma and other diseases. These problems were exacerbated because few institutions existed in pre-state Palestine that could deal with their plight. Unable to depend on support from the nascent Jewish social organizations, or from the largely apathetic British government, the Zionist settlers turned inward and created their own forms of self-help, including a health fund. Because of their socialist orientation, mutual aid for Zionists meant that access to health and other services were to be based on an association to a labour-affiliated group.

The main accomplishment of the labour movement was the establishment of the *Histadrut*, the General Federation of Hebrew Workers in Palestine (now the General Federation of Workers in Israel) in 1920 (Pruess, 1965). Apart from its labour activities, the *Histadrut* was also involved in a host of economic, social and cultural activities not normally associated with a trade union. For example, the *Histadrut* was involved in land settlement, work contracts, vocational training, absorption of immigrants, and the promotion of Hebrew language and culture. In addition, the *Histadrut* was immersed in providing public works projects; the distribution of unemployment relief and social assistance; medical insurance and health services; housing, bank, savings and credit funds; youth organizations; theatre; and welfare, unemployment and disability funds. Membership in the labour federation was a prerequisite for gaining access to health services. Only *Histadrut* members could receive public health services, and non-affiliated citizens were denied access even if they wished to pay (this limitation has since been abolished). Thus, the *Histadrut* was both a labour union and a workers commonwealth (*Chevrat Ovdim*) (Lucas, 1975).

Concurrent with the creation of the *Histadrut*, the Manufacturers' Association (the central organ of private industry) was established in 1925 as a bank and import firm. With the rise of urban centres, private industry and the influx of capital in the mid-1930s, the trade union struggle became more pressing. In opposition to the socialist tendencies in the worker-owned industries (where salaries were based on family needs rather than specialization), the private sector used the usual criteria of economic and professional competence as the basis for wages (Eisenstadt, 1967). As a result of the strong connection between service provision and labour affiliation, the private sector was forced to develop alternative sick funds and pension funds.

By 1935 a coherent and centralized political leadership emerged under the framework of the British mandate. This Jewish self-government gained legislative recognition by the British through the National Council (the self-governing organ of Jews in Palestine) and the Jewish Agency (Lucas, 1975). Because the Zionists abhorred charity, the delivery of personal social services was provided mainly by the *Vaad Leumi* (National Council) and the *Sochnut* (Jewish

Agency). Social services were delivered and administered locally in almost every community, and they were provided regardless of political affiliation, social status or ethnic origin. Although extensive, the local social services were not designed to replace private voluntary social welfare organizations such as *Hadassah*, ORT, American Mizrachi Women and various youth organizations. Instead, local social services were designed to coordinate and supervise the activities of the voluntary agencies.

While the basic philosophy was that social services should be provided on a state-based model (*Mamlachtiut*) (Jefet, 1954), questions remained as to how much of this complicated service structure should be carried over to the post-independence period. Meeting the goal of *Mamlachtiut* required patterning governmental infrastructures in a way that most closely resembled a normal state structure. Therefore, with the creation of the State of Israel the bulk of services originally provided by voluntary organizations were subsequently funded or delivered by government. While this arrangement complied with the socialist values of the *Histadrut* and the workers parties, it conflicted with the values of the capitalistic private sector. Ben-Gurion, the founding father of the State of Israel and a supporter of *Mamlachtiut*, remarked: 'During the British mandate the *Histadrut* carried out *Mamlachti* functions because there were no other tools available. But now this would be a serious default of the state' (Ben-Gurion, 1959, p. 67). However, Ben-Gurion also believed that while the provision of social services was a state responsibility, its delivery could be done by third parties.

In practice, all sides agreed to state-provided services only in those areas where no established alternative service existed. This approach was not always engineered along strict ideological or party lines. For example, the *Histadrut* opposed transferring the sick fund to the state, while they supported state responsibility for work accident benefits. The radical right objected to transferring work accident benefits to the state, but they supported a national health insurance law. The reason for this inconsistency was that the *Histadrut* owned an extensive health care service, which the radical right was lacking. On the other hand, the radical right owned insurance companies, an enterprise in which the left was not involved. Thus, when partisan interests were endangered, self-preservation took precedence over ideological beliefs and a national health law was never passed (about 80 per cent of the Israeli population is currently insured with the *Histadrut*'s *Kupat*

Holim). Nevertheless, the *Mamlachtiut* approach triumphed and was embodied in the national insurance law, a victory that occurred because of the persistence of the governmental bureaucracy over party opposition (Doron, 1975).

Mamlachtiut was not a pressing issue when it came to the provision of personal social services. In fact, only the *Vaad Leumi*, and later the state, was interested in providing personal social services. Public assistance was felt to be in direct conflict with the Zionist ideals of self-reliance. Furthermore, one could not expect to build a socialist and Zionist nation when dependency was officially sanctioned (Schindler, 1980). As a reflection of this ideological ambivalence, the social service portfolios are usually distributed to the weakest parties in a coalition government.

The ideas of the *New Right* in Europe and America found rich ground in the antecedents of the modern Israeli welfare state. For one, the pioneers' almost puritanical emphasis on work complemented the radical right's belief in work as the ultimate provider of economic security. Second, a basic goal of the movement is to separate the state provision of social services from state financing. In the peculiar history of Israel, that separation was built into the structure of services before independence. For example, unlike most modern welfare states, Israel does not have a true national health service, relying instead on quasi-public health providers such as the *Histadrut*. Using the quasi-public *Histadrut* as the primary health care provider may make privatizing social services appear less daunting. In the end, the historical threads that bind the modern Israeli state also fosters the populist basis of radical right ideas.

The modern Israeli welfare state

The Israeli welfare state is composed of three main components: income maintenance programmes (including commodity subsidization), social insurance and personal social services. In American welfare terminology, the Israeli welfare state can be understood as a 'mixed welfare economy' (Kamerman, 1983). In other words, it is an amalgamation of state, private non-profit and labour-sponsored social welfare institutions and programmes.

A major component of the Israeli welfare state is the *Bituach Leumi* (the National Insurance Institute). Developed as a national social insurance plan, the quasi-public *Bituach Leumi* encompasses a wide range of social insurance programmes, including: old age and survivors' insurance, long-term care benefits, disability benefits, rehabilitation benefits, income support benefits, alimony, child allowances (currently paid for the second child and beyond), maternity benefits, employment and accident injury benefits, benefits for casualties of hostile actions, benefits for reserve military service (a portion of a military reservist's salary is paid while they are on active duty), unemployment benefits, insurance of employees in cases of bankruptcy or the winding-up of corporate bodies, and legal aid. All supplemental income maintenance payments for low-income families or individuals are paid through *Bituach Leumi*. In short, the national insurance institute functions both as a social insurance and a means-tested income support programme. Unlike rigid social insurance programmes, many benefit programmes under *Bituach Leumi* are not strictly linked to past or current employment.

Health care is provided to Israelis through membership in one of the existing health care insurance funds (the largest is *Kupat Holim* of the *Histadrut*). These health funds provide comprehensive health care and are free at the point of entry. *Bituach Leumi* covers the costs of health insurance for low-income persons who receive supplemental income payments.

Apart from providing personal social services and income maintenance benefits, the Israeli government also provides commodity subsidization. Government subsidization occurs through two avenues: the subsidization of basic foodstuffs and the subsidization of public transportation. The main subsidized foodstuffs include bread, milk, eggs, poultry, and edible oil and margarine. The government subsidizes public transportation through the subsidization of bus fares.

Personal social services are funded and delivered by government and private non-profit organizations. For example, *Na'amat* (the *Histadrut* women's organization) operates day care centres; *Hadassah*, an American women's organization, funds and operates the largest and most modern hospital in Israel; AMIT operates shelters for abused women and children; ORT and WIZO operate vocational training centres; and AKIM operates homes and services for the mentally retarded. Although these organizations are voluntary, much of their funding comes from governmental sources. In summary, Israeli social services represent a mixed economy with a rich blend of private and public service providers.

Although the social welfare coverage of Jewish Israelis is generally typical of Western industrial nations, it is marked by a form of institutional discrimination. For example, while Israel's Proclamation of Independence (1948) declares that the state 'will ensure complete equality of social and political rights to all its inhabitants irrespective of religion, race, or sex' (Israel, Office of Information, 1948), in reality the precepts of Zionism often conflict with the realities of a multicultural state. Consequently, most of Israel's non-Jewish population lack the same personal social service coverage as the Jewish population.

For example, the infrastructure and services in Arab–Israeli towns are noticeably less developed than in Jewish areas. Arab–Israeli towns often have poor roads, inadequate sanitation and inferior schools. This explains, in part, why only 10 per cent of the non-Jewish population pass their high school matriculation examinations compared to 25 per cent of Jewish Israelis (the illiteracy rate among non-Jews is almost 37 per cent compared to 9 per cent for Jews). Moreover, although non-Jews account for over 16 per cent of Israel's population, only 4 per cent are represented among undergraduates. This discrimination also accounts for significant economic inequalities. For example, almost 74 per cent of non-Jewish households are in the lower income decile compared to 26 per cent of Jewish households (Cnaan, 1985, p. 67). The pattern of inequality also extends to the professional manpower allocation in social services, where Jewish communities have 173 social workers per 154,000 compared to 64 social workers for 156,000 residents in non-Jewish communities (Cnaan, 1985, p. 67).

Many key social welfare benefits in Israel are linked to participation in military service. For example, veterans are given preference in student loans, are entitled to veteran's aid and higher child allowances, and receive various other social benefits. However, while most Jews must undergo compulsory military service, most non-Jews are exempt. As such, more than 83 per cent of Jewish families with three or more children are veteran's aid recipients, compared to 16.5 per cent of non-Jewish families. In short, because many key welfare benefits are linked to military service, there is implicit discrimination against those minorities (including ultra-orthodox Jews who are also exempt from military service) who do not enter Israel's armed forces (Cnaan, 1985). Taken together, these factors point to a pattern of institutional inequality in the Israeli welfare state.

The ascendancy of the radical right in Israel

To investigate the impact of the Israeli radical right on the welfare state, it is important to explore its recent popularity. The rise to power of the Israeli right in the 1970s did not follow the same path as in other industrial nations, such as Britain and the United States. Overall, three factors led to the *Likud*'s rise to power in 1977.

First, the triumphant ecstasy of the Six Day War gave way to the disillusionment and fear of the Yom Kippur War of 1973. Unlike the swift victory of the Six Day War in 1967, the 1973 surprise attack by Egypt and Syria found Israel unprepared, and its margin of victory was far narrower than in 1967. Frightened by this close call, many Israelis blamed Labour and then Prime Minister Golda Meir for the lack of preparedness of the political, military and security agencies.

Second, the Labour Party was perceived by many Israelis as having bled the economy through corruption, nepotism and incompetence. Lastly, in contradiction to the myth that Israel is a nation of displaced Europeans, over 50 per cent of Israelis are Sephardic (Oriental) Jews, most from Arab-speaking countries. Most Sephardic Jews came to Israel in the early 1950s from Morocco, Yemen, Iraq, Iran, Syria, Libya and Egypt. Upon arrival, they found the social, political and economic institutions controlled by Ashkenazi (European) Jews. Because many Ashkenazis believed that Sephardic Jews came from a primitive Arab culture, various forms of political, social and economic discrimination became widespread (Yonah, 1990). In spite of their numerical majority, Oriental Jews make up only 17 per cent of university students, and their annual incomes are well below those of the Ashkenazi (Yonah, 1990). Although Israel's social welfare programmes were developed under Labour, the reaction against the élite Ashkenazi-dominated Labour Party led many of these angry Sephardic voters to defect *en masse* to *Likud* which, in turn, led to the electoral victory of Menachem Begin in 1977 and again in 1981.

Menachem Begin differed from conservative politicians in Western nations. Unlike Mr Reagan or Mrs Thatcher, Begin did not run on an avowedly capitalist plank of free enterprise and an end to government intervention in the marketplace. Needing to retain the support of his poorer constituency, Begin was not promoted as an adversary of the welfare state and, in fact, one of his electoral promises was to rebuild poor neighbourhoods in Israel, something that would have been anathema to either Reagan or Thatcher. Thus, the appeal of *Likud* was not based as much on *laissez-faire* economics as on populist rhetoric and a reaction to the political hegemony of the Labour Party.

Likud was unable to continue its majority rule after Begin stepped down in 1984, and was forced to share power in a coalition government with Labour. This national unity government was composed of the two giant parties — Labour and *Likud* — and smaller parties on both the left and the right. In 1988 neither Labour nor *Likud* could again garner a majority, and the coalition government was continued. By early 1990 the national unity government finally collapsed, and by a narrow margin the *Knesset* approved a conservative *Likud* government.

In contrast to Britain and the United States, *New Right* ideas did not wend their way into Israeli society through strong leaders. Instead, the fractured nature of Israeli political life precluded the emergence of a strong leader rooted in a national consensus. Even if conservative leaders like Yitzhak Shamir, Benny Begin, Ariel Sharon and Binyamin Netanyahu possessed a coherent economic vision, they lack the charisma, voter loyalty and party organization to carry out any far-reaching social or economic agenda. Nevertheless, the acceptance of radical right economic ideas filtered into Israeli society through several avenues, including a general frustration with a lacklustre economy and high inflation, the frustration of living in a society marked by constant labour unrest, the perceived inefficiencies in the Israeli economy, the anxiety of having to compete in a more competitive global economy, and the advice of conservative economic consultants such as Milton Friedman and Alvin Rabushka. These factors were strengthened by the strong political, historic and economic historic ties between Israel and the United States, and by the legions of Israelis who were influenced by their work and study in North America. Moreover, the perceived corruption and inefficiency in the *Histadrut* (which many people believe led to its virtual bankruptcy) and government-run industries contributed to a sense of urgency about the need for change. The fiscal crisis facing the *Histadrut* and government industries, and the pressures for economic change coming from US and foreign lending banks, made it difficult for Labour's old guard to defend the economic status quo. Lastly, radical right ideas were fuelled by the economic inferiority experienced by many Israelis and by Reagan's propaganda about the success of the US economy in the mid- and late-1980s. Taken together, it is not surprising that radical right economic thinking gained currency in Israeli society.

Radical right policies in Israel followed the same general pattern as in Britain and the United States. For example, during the mid-1980s Israel was faced with a staggering rate of inflation, which when annualized, reached 460 per cent in July 1985. In what could be described as a modern economic miracle, inflation was lowered by a coalition government of Labour and *Likud* (with Labour's Shimon Peres as the head of the Finance Ministry). The main strategy for combating inflation was based on traditional *New Right* solutions, including salary freezes (with the *Histadrut*'s consent) and cuts in public services and social welfare. As such, in July 1985 Israel began moving in a more conservative direction — lower marginal tax rates, expansion of the capital market base, minimizing the budget deficit and cutting governmental services (*The Israeli Economist*, 1989b).

Like other nations influenced by radical right ideas, the Israeli government began to stress economic individualism, which resulted in substantial cuts in public expenditures, attempts to cut levels of taxation, the privatization of the economy through selling off publicly held industries, and the creation of tax and spending policies that furthered the economic distance between upper and lower income brackets. For example, led by the former Labour-held Ministry of Finance, the government embarked on a rapid programme of privatization. Yossi Beilin, a former deputy finance minister and personal aide of Shimon Peres, advocates widespread industrial competition and the privatization of all government-held industries, including banks (Krivine, 1990). A recent headline in the *Jerusalem Post* read: 'Israeli Privatization — Gov't to Investors: It's All For Sale' (Kohn, 1990). Desperate for cash, the *Histadrut* is also trying to sell a large portion of its industrial empire, including the huge Koors Industries (Kohn, 1990).

Despite the influence of radical right ideas, there is no powerful political movement in Israel that can be labelled as a *New Right* party in the British or American sense. Instead, radical right thinking has permeated both Labour and *Likud*. For example, Labour Party leader Shimon Peres controlled the Finance Ministry during the fight against inflation, and it can be argued that he bears major responsibility for the deep cuts in commodity subsidization and social welfare programmes. Moreover, in examining the policies of the Labour-controlled Finance Ministry during the 1980s, it can also be argued that Peres was one of the leading architects of radical right thinking in Israel.

Because of their fluid political constituencies, both *Likud* and Labour have had to modify their economic position. Since *Likud*'s strength never laid in the white-collar vote, but in many of Israel's poorer neighbourhoods, it was forced to become moderate on economic and social welfare issues. On the other hand, the Labour Party was forced to modify its socialist ideology because most of its traditional supporters had matured with the state of Israel, and instead of being rugged pioneers, they became successful businesspeople, professionals or highly placed government bureaucrats. Sam Lehman-Wilzig (1989) observes that:

> *Likud* has been in the forefront of recent social welfare populism . . . while 'Socialistic' Labour is run by a leader [Shimon Peres] who extols the virtues of high-tech industry.
>
> By the 1980s Labour's socialist ideology was no longer in the best interests of its constituency! What voters in the middle and upper class would want continued high progressive taxation, rigid large-scale unionization and massive commodity subsidization? Thus, Labour found itself . . . either abandoning its cherished socialist ideology or losing part of its traditional electorate. Its solution was ideological obfuscation.
>
> *Likud*, like Labour, woke up to find that its supporters were opposed to its economic ideology — the poorer Oriental Jews that made up a large portion of its support wanted *more* government services, regulations, subsidies, etc. *Likud* did like Labour — do one thing while talking another. (Lehman-Wilzig, 1989, p. 7)

The impact of the radical right on the Israeli welfare state

Throughout the 1980s, the pattern of social welfare expenditures in Israel followed the same general pattern as in other countries influenced by the radical right: deep budget cuts in personal and in-kind social services; the implementation of more restrictive criteria for means-tested welfare programmes; curtailing public consumption of social welfare; reduced governmental responsibility for public welfare, including deep cuts in universal programmes (e.g., commodity and transportation subsidization); attempts at separating government provision of social services from governmental financing, including efforts to privatize social services; and marked growth in the costs of statutory entitlement programmes. The Israeli welfare state also underwent considerable fluctuations in funding throughout the 1980s. These fits and spurts can be understood in terms of three specific periods: a decline in social service spending during 1983–4; a stabilization at the new, lower level in 1985–7; and renewed growth from 1988–9 (Kop, 1989).

A simple examination of the social welfare budget is not sufficient in understanding the radical right's true impact on the Israeli welfare state. For example, although the budget for Israel's social services grew in absolute terms (in 1988 prices it grew by over $1.5 billion) in the 1980s, over 80 per cent of this growth was in statutory income maintenance programmes. Since the mid-1980s real growth in income maintenance expenditures stood at 9 per cent per annum (Kop, Blankett and Sharon, 1988). Although Israel's social welfare budget grew by 1.2 per cent from 1980 to 1985, from 1985 to 1988 the pace picked up to 7.4 per cent per annum. This growth is partly explained by the supply-side oriented economic stabilization plan of 1985, which dislocated large groups in Israeli society, thus making them eligible for statutory income maintenance programmes. In that sense, the deep budget cuts of the 1980s actually increased rather than decreased Israeli public welfare expenditures.

When Israel's social welfare budget data are scrutinized, it shows a pattern similar to the United States and Britain. Taking population growth into account, there was diminished activity in the 1980s in areas that represent public consumption (e.g., education, health and personal welfare) in favour of a dispersal of allowances, which were privately used. For example, data on expenditures for in-kind services (almost exclusively education and health, with a small proportion of welfare services) indicate that in 1985–6 there was a cumulative decline of 7 per cent, on top of a previous decline of nearly 10 per cent in 1983–4. On the other hand, income maintenance services grew rapidly during the 1980s, with old age pensions and child allowances increasing by 57 per cent and 32 per cent, respectively. Much like in Britain and the United States, this increase did not result from greater governmental generosity, but from a growth in the rolls of inflation-sheltered and relatively well protected income maintenance programmes (Kop, Blankett and Sharon, 1988).

A watershed event occurred for the Israeli welfare state in the mid-1980s. In 1985, defence appropriations totalled 40 per cent of Israel's disposable national budget, more than any other sector. The social welfare slice of the budget was 32 per cent. By 1988 the tables had turned: social services claimed 41 per cent of the national budget, with defence trailing behind at 34 per cent (Kop, 1988). However, as mentioned earlier, much of this rise is attributable to the effects of statutory income maintenance programmes rather than real increases in in-kind or personal social services.

Several important changes occurred in the Israeli welfare state during the final years of the 1980s. Since July 1985 (when the economic stabilization programme was introduced), there has been a continuous trend toward reducing consumer subsidies on food and public transportation. After peaking in 1984, the subsidization budget dropped from a high of about $1.5 billion in 1984 to about $250 million in 1989. At the height of expenditures in 1984, consumer subsidies lowered the Gini coefficient (the yardstick of net income inequality) by 6 per cent; by 1986–7 (after significant cuts) consumer subsidies only lowered the Gini coefficient by 1.8 per cent (Ahdut and Sadka, 1989). These deep cuts in consumer subsidies are consistent with *New Right* thinking, since they diminish the responsibility of government to respond to the social welfare needs of the population. Perhaps more importantly, these cuts signify the abandonment of traditional ideas about the role of the Israeli welfare state in income redistribution. While compatible with the radical right's emphasis on economic individualism, these cuts in consumer subsidies have resulted in a deteriorated economic position for Israel's poor.

As part of the economic stabilization plan of 1985, the Israeli government discontinued payment of children's allowances for the first child in families of up to three children (the national insurance institute continues to reimburse low-income families for the first child). While hurting small families, the exemption for families with three or more children immunized large families from the hardship of the cuts. Interestingly, this proposal came out of the Labour-held Ministry of Finance rather than *Likud*. The provision excluding families with three or more children was politically based, since in Israel large families tend to be religious. Thus, the exemption for large families was indicative of the importance of religious parties in Israel's coalition governments.

In 1989 the Israeli Finance Ministry — in a move surpassing the boldness of even Ronald Reagan and Mrs Thatcher — proposed the abolition of free education. Specifically, if parents of children in grades 1–8 (elementary and middle school) earn more than $450 a person per month, they would be required to pay about $25 a month per child for up to three children (the fourth would be free). (For high-income families the payment could go as high as $50 per month for a child.) In other words, the minimum income for charging school fees for a family of four would be $1,800 per month (public education would be free below the minimum income). Whether or not this bill passes, the fact that it is being debated represents a profound shift in the concept of social welfare as a public utility.

In line with the radical right's focus on privatizing social services, the *Knesset* recently passed a nursing care bill which, for the first time, allows the government to reimburse private, for-profit providers of nursing care services. Although it is too early to assess whether this bill will lead to a burgeoning for-profit social welfare industry like in the United States, or whether it will be a precursor for other, more significant attempts at privatization, it represents a radical departure for the Israeli welfare state.

The overall pattern that emerged in the Israeli welfare state during the 1980s resembles the pattern of other nations influenced by radical right thinking. In particular, this pattern includes deep cuts in public welfare expenditures, attempts to privatize social services, the promulgation of bold initiatives designed to facilitate a governmental retreat from social welfare responsibilities, and an increase in expenditures for statutory social welfare programmes coupled with a decrease for in-kind and personal social services. In sum, these changes represent a significant retrenchment of governmental responsibility for social welfare.

Contrary to Western voters who enjoy peace, Israelis are greatly concerned with foreign policy issues, often at the expense of focusing on domestic economic concerns. The fierce struggles in Israel over 'land for peace', over the establishment of a Palestinian state on the West Bank and Gaza, and over an international conference on peace in the Middle East dominate public debates.

Despite this focus, Israel is in the midst of major social and economic changes. Saddled with a five year recession, a 9.3 per cent unemployment rate, huge defence and internal security costs, a massive and costly immigration of Russian Jewish refugees (which in four years will constitute a 25 per cent increase in the Israeli population) (Lipkis, 1990), and a foreign debt of over S16 billion, Israel is currently re-evaluating its social priorities.

Radical right pundits argue that governmental funding for the welfare state should be secondary to Israel's survival in a highly competitive global economy. They argue that because Israel is a small nation with a limited domestic market and few natural resources, it is highly dependent on foreign trade. Conservatives maintain that Israel must modernize, recapitalize and rationalize its industrial structure if it is to survive in a competitive international marketplace. Radical right supporters (as well as many moderate politicians) argue that the process of economic rationalization implies strong limits on governmental spending, a highly productive labour force and the freeing-up of money for investment. In that sense, the control exerted by Israel's radical right is best illustrated by its ability to shape the debate around the economic agenda of the country, regardless of which party is in power.

Major challenges to the welfare state will undoubtedly increase as Israel is forced to survive in a highly competitive world economy. Moreover, welfare debates will likely be overshadowed by the economic exigencies facing Israel. Given this scenario, the left is as likely to cut welfare benefits as the right. There is, of course, always the possibility that a more creative avenue will be found that increases economic productivity while ensuring the adequacy of welfare benefits. This is the task facing Israel and the rest of the industrialized world.

8

Caught in the middle: the radical right and the Canadian welfare state

Ernie Lightman

Canada has never embraced neo-conservative or *New Right* ideology with the enthusiasm of Thatcher's Britain or Reagan's America. At the same time the Canadian welfare state, particularly since the onset of monetarism in the mid-1970s, has come under severe attack. The result has been a fundamental restructuring (Lightman and Irving, 1991) of the gains achieved through nearly half a century of struggle. This retreat has not primarily been based on ideology, at least on the surface, for radical right rhetoric has a singularly alien tone when applied in the Canadian context. Instead, the case to dismantle Canada's welfare state has been argued largely in terms of fiscal capacity and the need to reduce structural deficits within a federal budgetary process.

This chapter examines retreat within the Canadian welfare state. It begins with an analysis of the changing nature of federalism and then proceeds to an overview of Canada's achievements beginning in the immediate post-Second World War period. The high point of Canada's welfare state was reached in 1971 and subsequently there has followed retrenchment and decline, a process of gradual chipping away at the outset, followed in more recent years by an acceleration, as the chips become chunks, with even the occasional big block. The chapter concludes with an evaluation of what are the distinguishing characteristics of Canada's somewhat reluctant embrace of the *New Right* and an assessment of why these features should have emerged in the way they did.

Canada: the importance of federalism

In a recent article on Canadian political ideology, Gibbins and Nevitte observed:

> It may be the case that Canadian political life has been dominated by such issues as the Constitution, federal provincial relations, the place of Quebec within the Canadian community, western alienation, issues that are not easily or traditionally organized through a left–right optic . . . there has been neither need nor opportunity for Canadians to structure their political world along conventional ideological lines. (Gibbins and Nevitte, 1985, p. 598)

What this analysis implies is that to understand Canada one must understand federalism, more than ideology. The role of the state throughout Canadian history has been expressed primarily through the dynamic of nation building and capital accumulation; the role of ideology, as expressed through partisan politics, has been secondary, with few and minor substantive differences between the two major political parties. It is necessary, therefore, to begin this chapter not with information on standards of living or social indicators — for Canada is clearly a wealthy country by any criterion — but rather with a brief foray into the murky waters of Canadian federalism.

At the country's birth in 1867 Canada was intended to be a highly centralized federation, but time and court interpretations have reversed this. To Ottawa were originally given unlimited taxing powers, while the provinces received exclusive responsibility for service delivery areas including health, education and welfare. While these latter were relatively unimportant a century ago they have, of course, become significant over time. The result was an ever-growing imbalance, in which the provinces had major service responsibilities but lacked the resource base to meet these, while Ottawa had the fiscal capacity but only a limited delivery role. Particularly since the 1950s, Canadian social and political history has been marked by a series of complex federal/provincial arrangements to offset the early constitutional imbalances — tax rentals and tax sharing arrangements; equalization payments to aid the poorer provinces and regions; and rather creative incentives by Ottawa to lead the provinces where it wished them to go — cost sharing in areas such as social assistance/dole or medicare in which Ottawa pays 50 per cent of the bill if the provinces meet specified federal conditions.

Fiscal complexity has always been compounded by the constitutional question of Quebec's place within the federation. In many ways this issue was the central — some would say the sole — preoccupation of the Trudeau years (1968–84 with one minor break in 1979). Trudeau's work culminated in the Canada Act 1982, which patriated the Canadian Constitution for the first time, but was achieved only without the signature of Quebec which could not accept the limits imposed on its sovereignty.

A pro-separatist provincial government had been elected in Quebec in 1976, and in 1980 a referendum was held on sovereignty-association, a weak form of separation. This, however, was defeated. The decade of the 1980s was preoccupied in Canada with finishing Trudeau's uncompleted business and bringing Quebec into the Constitution, a process which culminated in a 1987 agreement known as the Meech Lake Accord.

Ratification of the Accord was required by all ten provincial legislatures by 23 June 1990, a goal which was not met. It is indeed significant that the Accord was ultimately blocked by representatives of two of the most marginalized groups in Canadian society — one native Canadian in the Manitoba legislature, and the premier of Newfoundland who correctly saw the Accord as severely weakening the central authority in Canada, a process which could only work to the detriment of poorer regions such as his own.

Fiscal and constitutional issues come together through a changing perception inside Quebec as to whether federalism pays. For many years Quebec governments had been guided by the principle of *le federalisme comptable* or profitable federalism, a phrase closely associated with the provincial premier, Robert Bourassa. The expression described a situation in which Quebec was a net beneficiary of federal government spending, in that federal expenditures in Quebec exceeded the tax revenues generated for Ottawa within the province. By 1990, however, the federal preoccupation with deficit reduction had lowered or even eliminated Quebec's 'profit' from the federal state. At the same time, reports from a number of New York investment houses claimed that an independent Quebec would be economically viable on its own. A new confident business entrepreneurial class had emerged within Quebec which was committed to a form of business nationalism which could best be achieved through separation.

In light of the failure to ratify Meech Lake, it is clear that the 1990s will portend a continuing crisis within the Canadian federal state.

This tension is further exacerbated by the signing of the Free Trade Agreement between Canada and the United States which took effect in January 1989. Unlike the European single market, the Canada–United States agreement entails free movement of goods and some services but not of people. Among the fears of many Canadians were that free trade would entail a massive downward levelling of occupational benefits as Canadian employers rush to compete with the non-unionized low wage and low tax states in the American south; Canadians would be left in low wage job ghettos feeding the large American market from the outside (Drache, 1990; Social Planning Council, 1988). There was also considerable opposition to the specific terms of the free trade agreement — that it was simply a bad deal for Canada. Canadian fears were further increased by the announcement in mid-1990 that the United States and Mexico were about to engage in their own free trade negotiations.

The free trade agreement itself had been endorsed in the 1988 federal election, a one issue referendum style contest. Though the governing Conservatives who alone advocated the plan were supported by only 42 per cent of the voters, Canada's three-party system yielded a workable majority in the House of Commons. The agreement had been opposed by every community-based social welfare interest group in the country along with labour, anti-poverty groups, women's groups and environmentalists. Support for the agreement came from the conservative constituency of the rich, the large corporations both national and multinational, and the associated business groups (Warnock, 1988). The *New Right* as such was not a prominent player, but since the Agreement was presented as reinforcing the market, it is fair to assume most of the *New Right* constituency was on the pro side. The polarity within Canada around free trade was clear for all to see and perhaps for the first time in Canadian history the issues were openly argued on class lines (Campbell, 1988). The election campaign itself was fraught with emotion with the leader of the Liberal opposition symbolically wrapping himself in the Canadian flag and business leaders threatening mass layoffs should the agreement be rejected. Millions of dollars were spent in saturation media advertising on the part of the pro-agreement groups.

The Conservatives had presented the agreement as entailing short-term pain for long-term gain, and immediately upon the signing of the treaty the pain began. Firms closed their Canadian operations and proceeded to supply the small Canadian market from their

American factories while maintaining only local distribution outlets north of the border. Though it is difficult to separate out agreement-related unemployment from cyclical and other forms of job loss, the major anti-free trade group estimated as a minimum a loss of 70,000 jobs during the first year of the treaty's operation (Howard, 1990). Earlier government promises of massive worker adjustment programmes were completely abandoned and even the unemployment compensation system which might have provided some cushion was severely cut back in the name of fiscal restraint.

The free trade agreement is also central to understanding the future of Canada's welfare state because it contained a prohibition on government subsidies which were henceforth to be viewed as forms of unfair competition. These same subsidies, however, have always been the essence of much social policy activity within Canada. Just what constitutes a subsidy was not spelled out in the agreement because the two countries were unable to reach a consensus; interpretation of the term was left to be resolved over a period of seven years. Many US subsidies to industry are hidden in defence procurement contracts, an area specifically excluded from the scope of the treaty. In Canada, however, subsidies are open, visible and politically important (Drover, 1988).

Throughout its history, Canada has always been marked by an active interventionist government, certainly in contrast to the experience in the United States (Panitch, 1977). It has only been through major government involvement in daily personal and business life that an east–west country has been moulded and maintained in the face of the overwhelming logic of north–south communications: people in the Atlantic provinces have always had more in common with the New England states than with the rest of Canada, and the residents of British Columbia along with their counterparts in Oregon and California often seem to forget that the world does extend east of the ski resorts in the Rocky Mountains.

In some ways the primary role of the Canadian federal state (and more specifically the governing party in Ottawa) has always been to reconcile the divergent interests in order to hold the country together. Regional subsidies, local area grants and the like have always been central to the Canadian political scene as was the general acceptance of local job creation programmes and other forms of direct government spending. The regions have tended to respond to these spending initiatives in electoral terms, such that regional economic ests and blocks of parliamentary votes are intimately linked with another. Quebec was perhaps the most skilled in this art with its *federalisme comptable*, but the prairie farmers and Atlantic fishermen have never been far behind (Savoie, 1990). Indeed, one of the early implications of the failure of the Meech Lake Accord may be to accentuate even further the self-interested activity of each province and provincial government; the concept of a national interest seemed at risk of fading into the background.

Federal elections in Canada are won not primarily on the basis of ideology or policy, for the two major parties differ in these areas only to a slight degree. Victories are achieved on the relative ability of the two major parties to satisfy the large and well-organized voting blocks in the different regions representing the different interests within the country: in the 1988 election, for example, Quebec voted massively for the Conservatives, and without the votes of Quebec the treaty would have gone down to ignominious defeat.

Returning to the comments of Gibbins and Nevitte, it is clear that the radical right within the Canadian context cannot simply be viewed as an extreme endpoint along some left–right continuum. At the federal level at least brokerage politics — the ability to satisfy various interest groups, most of which are organized on regional linguistic and developmental lines — remains the key to electoral success. At the same time, Ottawa does represent more than just a broker among competing interest groups: throughout the country's history it has been central as an active promoter of economic development (and, often as a by-product, of social development as well). At the same time, preoccupation with issues such as federal provincial relations, fiscal transfers and constitution making have simply left Ottawa no place on its complex agenda for an ideological purity of the radical right variety.

The Canadian welfare state: expansion and contraction

Within an international context, Canada is usually identified, alongside the United States, as being firmly within the residual camp: at the very least the similarities between the two North American countries are seen as more pronounced than any difference between either of them and any of the other major Western countries to which comparison is typically made (Kaim-Caudle, 1973; Coughlin, 1980; Banting, 1987). At the same time, this does not imply that the distinctions between Canada and the United States are unimportant or trivial (O'Connor, 1989). In place of the Lockeian liberalism of its southern neighbour and the associated ideological aversion to government, Canada's history has been marked by an active and interventive state.

Although the ravages of the Great Depression of the 1930s led to some early government involvement in Canadian economic and social life, the end of the Second World War really marked the beginning of the modern welfare state. The year 1943 saw the issuance of the Marsh Report, Canada's counterpart to Beveridge, written by Oxford-trained and Keynes-influenced public servants (Canada, 1945). The Marsh Report endorsed notions of demand management, deficit financing and countercyclical stabilization policy. Although its approach was employment based and overtly redistributive policies were not considered, the report did legitimate notions of direct government involvement in the economy. Canada's family allowance programme, the universal non-contributory child benefit, was introduced at this time.

Influenced by developments in Britain the decade of the 1950s saw many additions to Canada's welfare state: blind and disability pensions; a universal non-contributory payment known as old age security (OAS); unemployment assistance; and hospital insurance. Taken together, the family allowance and old age security programmes have come to represent the twin pillars of universal entitlement in Canada's welfare state. Through the years they have acquired a symbolism of commitment to an active and benevolent social policy that has provided an ideological focus for radical right opposition, although in the case of family allowances the amounts of money involved are quite small.

The 1960s saw the last three major building blocks in the Canadian welfare state: the Canada Pension Plan (1965) was a universal and mandatory government-run and employment-based contributory pension plan, intended to supplement the universal entitlement of OAS. The Canada Assistance Plan, 1966, represents the country's major social assistance/dole legislation: provided that certain federal conditions are met, Ottawa pays half the cost of the provincial social assistance bills.

The final pillar and, in many ways the crown of Canada's welfare state, was the 1966 passage of the medicare legislation. This programme entailed universal and free (at the point of use) medical care for insured services which included virtually all care within a hospital setting as well as most visits to private medical practitioners.

The election of Pierre Trudeau as Liberal party leader and Prime Minister in 1968 shifted Ottawa's focus away from social policy development and in the direction of constitutional matters. In fact, notwithstanding his international image as a progressive, little of substance emerged in the social policy arena during the Trudeau years, largely because of his own fundamental disinterest in this area. There was a major expansion of the unemployment insurance system in 1971 which introduced extended maternity benefits and an expanded regional element, but these changes were largely the achievement of the minister responsible. With the 1971 amendments, unemployment insurance moved from a nominally actuarily-based insurance programme to a central pillar of the social welfare system and a major component of the government's regional policy programme.

The year 1971 also saw the release of a major Senate report on poverty in Canada (SPRG, 1971). Undoubtedly influenced by the various wars on poverty occurring south of the border through the decade of the 1960s and the associated anti-Vietnam war sentiment, Canada's report highlighted, perhaps for the first time, the existence and extent of poverty within the country. As a result, the focus of social policy discussion began to shift away from the employment-based strategy of Marsh and more in the direction of overtly downwardly redistributive policies.

Decline began in Canada as elsewhere with the 1973 world oil crisis and the allied recession. Canada's response was through traditional Keynesian pump-priming and an increased deficit. The oil crisis also brought with it substantial imported inflation which was largely beyond the scope of a simple national response. This imported inflation was reinforced by deficits which resulted from Ottawa's attempts to spend its way out of recession: much spending at this time was indirect through tax expenditures and the automatic indexation of direct cash and tax benefits. By 1975 the Bank of Canada had begun to adopt the same strict monetarist policies as were being introduced elsewhere in the Western world (Wolfe, 1984). Since that day, to the present, Canada has been a high interest rate country: responsibility for social policy has truly shifted from the federal department of health and welfare to the federal department of finance and perhaps even more to the nominally independent Bank of Canada. For the last fifteen years the operative language in the social policy arena has been that of restraint, cutback, inflation control and deficit reduction. Aside from an initial ideological premise that inflation control should or must be the pre-eminent goal of government policy, all subsequent action has been couched in technical economistic language: government, it is claimed, has not necessarily desired to cutback the welfare state but rather such moves are necessary in the greater battle against inflation. Even the initial premise itself is not presented as a normative choice but rather as a self-evident truth essential for the survival of capitalism in a small export dependent economy.

Two major developments have marked the last fifteen years in Canadian social policy. The first of these, the refundable child tax credit, was introduced in 1978 and has been viewed as the only identifiable social policy advance since 1971. Because of the nominally progressive basis of personal income taxation in Canada, tax relief in the form of deductions is regressive in impact, being of a greater absolute value the greater one's income. The refundable child tax credit was the first programme to offer a fixed lump sum payment rather than an enhanced deduction and as such was relatively progressive and of greater value to the poor. Furthermore, the credit was refundable, unlike other forms of tax relief, so that a single mother could receive her benefit even if she paid no tax (NCW, 1978).

The other major entry to Canada's social welfare scene after 1975 was the foodbank, a voluntary sector non-governmental response to widespread hunger. Though the idea was imported from the United States, the Canadian foodbanks have seen their existence as anomalous and anachronistic, reminiscent of the soup kitchens of the Great Depression. Most look forward with both anger and anticipation to the day when they can self-destruct and government will assume its proper role of feeding the hungry (Riches, 1986).

The world recession of 1981 led to a substantial jump in Canada's deficit as the federal government again tried to spend its way to economic recovery. In addition, the economy by now contained numerous automatic stabilizers, primary among which was the relatively generous programme of unemployment insurance.

The election of the Conservative government under Brian Mulroney in 1984 represented a turning point in Canada's history, though it was perhaps not fully recognized as such at the time. The election campaign had been marked by few ideological differences between the two major parties as both vowed support for the welfare state: Mulroney, at one point, described old age security as a 'sacred trust' for his party, hyperbole he was later to regret. The Conservative victory resulted more from the disillusionment with the legacy of the Trudeau years, the failure of Trudeau's successor to carve out a clear image or set of policies, and the success of Mulroney in capturing the voters of Quebec as a 'native son'.

Once in office the government released an agenda for economic renewal which identified deficit reduction as a pre-eminent concern, a goal to be achieved through spending cuts rather than through increased taxation. This document represented perhaps the clearest statement of a radical right-wing philosophy ever produced by a federal governing party in Canada, though it was not ideologically pure: social policy innovations were to continue, said the document, but henceforth they would emerge as a by-product of economic growth and not as a result of overtly downwardly redistributive policies. The agenda has remained to the present day as the most explicit statement of ideological intent on the part of the Conservatives, the benchmark against which all subsequent actions have been measured by its critics on the right. The goal of cutting spending in preference to increased taxation as a means to deficit reduction has remained particularly elusive as we shall see, and as such it has been the source of much criticism from the *New Right*.

The organized expression of radical right-wing thought in Canada is limited to a small number of groups and individuals. Prominent among these is the Fraser Institute based in Vancouver and following the ideas of London's Institute of Economic Affairs (IEA). The Fraser Institute commissions research from 'approved' academics and does its own in-house work as well: the conclusions are inevitably *New Right* focused and ideologically 'pure', based on a belief in the market and in reducing the role of government. Calls for user fees as a way to ration and restrict abuse of medicare are a common theme, though there is little public or political support. Indeed, much of the Fraser Institute's material reads as if it had been written by the IEA, with changes only to the names of individuals and geographic locations. The true impact of the Fraser Institute on government policy is, however, unclear and controversial because of personal networks among individuals at the Institute, within the Conservative party, and in the federal bureaucracy (Langille, 1989). Mendelson (1987) has observed that, compared to both the United States and Britain, 'explicitly articulated extremism' is more difficult to find in Canada, though these views 'have also attracted a large following in Canada'.

The Conservative government's first budget, 1984, contained a lifetime exemption from taxation for capital gains of $500,000. This move was defended by no independent observer as serving any legitimate economic or social purpose, but was seen solely as a regressive reward to the Conservatives' upper income constituency. Though this provision was later reduced to $100,000, presumably after it had been fully utilized by all those with the resources to do so, it remains to this day as a symbol of upper income privilege. The budget simultaneously proposed the partial de-indexation of old age security and family allowances, a process by which payments in future would be increased only for that portion of inflation in excess of 3 per cent (i.e. there would be a real decrease of up to 3 per cent per year). Because the payments were to be reduced for all recipients — rich and poor alike — the proposal was seen as highly punitive to Canada's seniors, most of whom were poor. A grass roots spontaneous mobilization of the elderly led to demonstrations on Parliament Hill and calls to the Prime Minister to remember his sacred trust. The government was forced to ultimately retreat on OAS, though the cuts to family allowances remained.

Policy surrounding family allowances and old age security in Canada has always been symbolically important, for these universal benefits are viewed by both supporters and critics as central to the welfare state and its notions of legitimacy and entitlement. 'Does the Prime Minister's banker need family allowances?' was a widely posed question in 1984. The answers were presented within a context of increasing conservatism and budgetary crisis: the Prime Minister's banker, who was presumably a male, did not in fact receive family allowance, but rather the money went to his wife, and as such welfare state cutbacks were increasingly becoming a women's issue; furthermore, it was argued on efficiency grounds that it was preferable to deliver universally and recover selectively through the tax system, since the payments were taxable. If insufficient revenues were generated, the problem lay in a personal income tax system that was not sufficiently progressive.

The trend of the times, however, was in the direction of less rather than more progressive income taxation. Following tax reform in the United States, the Conservative government in 1987 introduced a two-part system of tax reform. The first, following other international actions, was presented as simplifying the personal income tax system by reducing the number of marginal brackets from ten to three and lowering the top tax rate simultaneously. The effect was to reduce taxation levels generally and particularly for the rich who were already doing quite well from the Conservatives. The National Council on Welfare (1989) estimated that, during the Conservatives' first term in office (1984–8), a typical low income household — the working poor — experienced an increase in real taxation of 44 per cent; for a middle income family real taxes grew by 10.2 per cent, while a typical upper income family faced a decline of 5.9 per cent in real taxes over the same time period. A 'report card' on the Conservatives' first term, issued by a coalition of six social policy interest groups, found that beyond these benefits already accruing to the rich, tax reform 'will provide token benefits to many poor Canadians and large benefits to the wealthy' (SPRG, 1988).

The second phase of tax reform due for introduction on 1 January 1991 was to be a goods and services tax (GST), a value added tax to replace the older manufacturer's sales tax. The latter is a narrowly based tax on manufactured goods only, similar in many ways to the old British purchase tax. Debate over the goods and services tax was to occupy much of 1990 in Canada.

A child care bill, introduced into the Commons in 1988, was intended to show the government's human side — a response to the crisis in child care and the growing needs of the now dominant two-wage owner household. Every group to testify at the Hearings stage criticized the bill and its market bias; it gave tax relief to parents (and as such was regressive in impact) and also assumed that parents as consumers were competent judges of quality without further need for government regulation. The House rose for the 1988 election with only the tax provisions enacted into law — a maximum tax saving of $1,643 per year for an upper income earner and an increase of $200 to the poor.

In the course of the 1988 'free trade' election the usual grandiose spending promises were made by all parties. The Conservatives, for example, offered over $5 billion to subsidize energy megaprojects in the west and off the Newfoundland coast, projects which would otherwise not be economically viable. Immediately after the election, the government 'discovered' a fiscal crisis: the federal deficit, and even more the accumulated debt, were now defined as being fundamentally out of control. Drastic action supported by a massive publicity campaign was now called for by the Conservatives in order to reduce the deficit and over time to run down the total debt. During the course of the election campaign itself, the debt had received scarcely a mention.

In early 1989 the government announced major changes to the unemployment insurance system, including an end to the government contribution directed towards the broader redistributive goals. The 1989 budget slashed government subsidies to the national passenger rail system which led to the closing of approximately half the rail service in the country. In addition, a form of clawback was now imposed on family allowance and old age security payments: the monthly benefits would continue to be received by all eligible Canadians but those above an income threshold would pay back, through the personal income tax system, the benefits received, up to a maximum of the total payment. The use of clawback was astute on the government's part: whereas its earlier attack on these payments in 1984 had been correctly seen as a reduction in the money to be received by the poor, the government was able to present its case in 1989 as reflecting progressive social policy. Only those with incomes above the threshold would pay back their benefits and this would occur on a sliding scale. The critics noted that the threshold was not indexed so that, over time, more and more recipients would be subject to clawback: 'People will pay, not because they are rich but because they are old' (Cohen and Lightman, 1989). Furthermore, critics noted the philosophical unacceptability of singling out selected elements of the tax system and recovering these at a higher rate, while the rest of the massive programme of tax relief was left untouched. The real problem once again was a tax system that was not sufficiently progressive.

This 1989 budget was unfortunately leaked to the press the day before its scheduled release. The opposition parties chose to ignore the substance of the budget and instead focused their attention on calls for the minister's resignation. These events, ultimately, were to the government's benefit for the budget was passed by the Commons with little discussion, the minister ignored calls for his resignation, and the parliamentary debating time never did really get around to the substance of the cutbacks.

A year later the 1990 budget was introduced at a much lower key, since the country was preoccupied with constitutional matters — the Meech Lake Accord — and the pending goods and services tax. The Prime Minister and his party at this time were at a record low of

15 per cent support as reported in the Gallup poll. Transfer payments to the richer provinces for the Canada Assistance Plan were now to be capped, subject to a ceiling for the first time and ending the open-ended 50 per cent federal contribution. The legislation itself, however, was untouched and so the effect was to shift fiscal responsibility from Ottawa to the provinces.

One relatively inexpensive item in the budget contained distinct traces of the punitive quality associated with the traditional radical right: during the Trudeau years the Prime Minister had personally believed in the importance of local community groups, people traditionally disempowered advocating before government on their own behalf. Federal funding had been introduced on a core or sustaining basis for a variety of women's, natives', anti-poverty and similar advocacy groups. In a context where government spending was always seen as 'normal' and expected, there was no ideological aversion in Canada to taking money from government to challenge this same government. For over twenty years these groups were important advocates on behalf of the less powerful within Canada. The 1990 budget severely cut this core funding to women's groups and natives: the amount of money involved was so slight that the action could only be interpreted as either ideologically based or simply reflecting a desire on the part of an increasingly unpopular government to silence its most vocal critics.

The prospect of closing vast numbers of women's shelters led to non-violent sit-ins in federal government offices across the country. The opposition released figures in the Commons showing that the government was to spend roughly half its projected savings on security guards to protect its offices against the sit-ins, and victory was in the air. The government restored roughly 75 per cent of the amount previously cut, though this was presented as a one time reinstatement ostensibly to give these groups lead time to secure alternative funding.

The last couple of years in Canada have been marked by great controversy about the goods and services tax and, to a lesser extent, the changes in unemployment insurance. In each case, the non-elected and Liberal party dominated Senate held up the government's legislation and threatened a constitutional crisis. Given the low popularity of the government and the divergence of practice from pre-election promise, the Senate felt on firm moral ground in exercising its constitutional authority to delay or even reject unpopular legislation. The GST in particular was seen as being particularly regressive in impact. It was also evidently the government's last chance to reduce its deficit. Attempts to cut direct spending had been singularly unsuccessful in a country where high government spending is structurally implanted. While the GST had been originally introduced as revenue neutral, this was quickly dismissed as even the massive government publicity acknowledged the GST would help in deficit reduction. Credits promised to the poor to offset the tax were dismissed as inadequate in amount and not indexed.

In short, then, the current status of Canada's welfare state may best be described as tenuous. No new programme initiatives have emerged in recent years, nor are any likely given the fiscal preoccupation with deficit reduction. At the federal level no party has overtly called for a *New Right* type programme, but dismantling of programmes has been justified on the grounds of fiscal necessity; indeed, the clawback of OAS and family allowances were even presented as progressive social changes. The constitutional crisis certain to emerge from the failure of the Meech Lake Accord will further complicate matters, as the traditional Canadian response of buying off the discontented does not seem probable. The final section of this chapter attempts to evaluate how and why Canada has achieved radical right outcomes in part, but only in part.

The radical right and the Canadian welfare state

Lightman and Irving (1991) have identified three features which characterize Canada's experience with neo-liberalism: the process began relatively late compared to the United States and Britain; it was marked by high taxation rather than reduced spending; and it was largely devoid of the rhetorical excesses of Reagan and Thatcher.

The absence of rhetoric may be subject to modification as the failure of the government to get its fiscal house in order by the 1990s became associated with increasingly strident language and action — constitutional crisis, the impact of free trade, and the punitive cutbacks in funding to women's and native groups. Furthermore, certain provincial governments — in particular those of British Columbia (Magnusson *et al.*, 1984) and Saskatchewan — have espoused radical right-wing thinking with all the fervour of a born again Thatcherite. Canada's provinces tend to be more homogeneous both economically and socially than is possible at a national level: the prairie governments are clear advocates for their farmers as the governments in the Atlantic region are for their fishermen (Stevenson, 1977). Furthermore, the western provinces developed later economically than did the rest of the country and, as such, were more subject to a direct political influence from the United States. This economic and social homogeneity, combined with the openness to American ideas, led to the emergence of relatively pure radical right rhetoric and ideology in at least two of the provinces. This has been expressed and defended as a normative statement of how life and the economy should be organized and not simply as the means to some technically superior outcome. Saskatchewan, in particular, was problematic for this province had always been the traditional home of Canadian socialism, the birthplace of medicare and much else. Riches (1990) has observed that this province has become 'a testing ground . . . it is clear that if the neo-conservative agenda can triumph in Saskatchewan, then it will have won a significant ideological battle'. As a provincial election approached in 1990, even the Conservative premier saw that his thoughts had not taken root in the rural agrarian and collectively inclined province. As a result, he began to pull back and major privatization plans were scrapped as the government increasingly thought in electoral terms (Pitsula and Rasmussen, 1990).

To the three factors identified by Lightman and Irving may be added a fourth characteristic, which would describe a fundamental ambivalence surrounding the national commitment to the welfare state and an associated reliance on technocratic explanations. The original conceptualization of the post-war welfare state in Canada did not entail an overtly redistributive approach. The welfare state was to be an adjunct to economic growth, one of a limited number of macroeconomic stabilizers built into the economy. In this, the approach follows the longer history of government involvement as promoting economic growth and development. Social programmes emerge as a by-product of economic growth or perhaps as a necessary precondition, but they were not seen as necessarily desirable in their own right. In O'Connor's (1973) language of functionalism, government social spending in Canada has always served an important accumulation function (Buchbinder, 1981). In this, the country stands apart from most other Western states where social spending serves a primary function of legitimation. Even the introduction of Canada's medicare programme in 1966 has been persuasively argued as meeting the goals of capital accumulation more than those of legitimation (Walters, 1982).

Central to underlying the attack on Canada's welfare state, however, has been the continued inability or unwillingness of Ottawa to reduce its overall spending. We have previously seen that active government activity to promote development has been one of the absolutely central features of Canadian economic and social history. This has translated into a political system based on interest group and area patronage, an electoral process in which votes are essentially bought through grandiose spending promises: to cut back spending potentially means to lose elections (Savoie, 1990).

Furthermore, there has developed through the years a sense of dependence on and acceptance of this spending by virtually all elements within the community. Traditional radical right hostility to government spending as morally improper has largely fallen on deaf ears in a society where self-reliance and independence from government have never had the same meaning as in the United States. Even the business lobby has displayed much ambivalence concerning government spending: prior to the 1990 budget, the idea was circulated widely that if Ottawa was serious about cutting spending it was now necessary to look at the system of massive industrial subsidies, many of which were hidden through tax expenditures. The Canadian Chamber of Commerce, for example, accepted in general and in principle the need to look at industrial subsidies, but the language is that of caution and there is never a readiness to identify specific areas, industries or firms (Fagan, 1990). Even regional policy which is probably illegal under free trade and is certainly incompatible with a market ethos which dictates that people should follow jobs rather than the reverse — even this is understood by business as keeping many marginal firms in operation and generating profits for shareholders. More generally, business groups understand the macroeconomic impact of government spending and the dangers of the withdrawal of purchasing power from an economy in times of low growth and high unemployment. In an interesting newspaper article prior to the 1990 budget, the president of the Canadian Chamber of Commerce argued that 'taking an axe to social programs would be cutting our own throats' (Reid, 1990). What he called for, in fact, was for social spending to be targeted as investment in human capital, in areas such as education and daycare. To use O'Connor's term again, the desire was that social spending be targeted to serve narrow accumulation purposes.

Even the goods and services tax is a final acknowledgement of Ottawa's inability to cut its spending: to the extent that the tax does succeed in reducing the deficit, it will do so only through massive increases in taxation and not through reducing government involvement. Canadians are thus faced with the paradoxical match of the political left and the radical right both opposing the GST, the former because of its generally regressive impact and the latter because it does not directly attack government spending.

Because of the government's fundamental inability to restrain its spending, tremendous reliance has been placed on monetary policy. The Bank of Canada operates at arm's length from the government of the day and has been assiduously following high interest rate policies since 1975 without a serious break. Because fiscal policy has remained partially expansionary, or at least not contractionary, monetary policy has been required to operate at an even more severe level than would otherwise have been the case. By assigning responsibility for tight money and high interest rates to the nominally independent Bank of Canada, the human and discretionary approach to spending restraint has been replaced in Ottawa by a seemingly objective neutral and dispassionate banking process, essentially beyond the scope of partisan politics.

High interest rates have, of course, slowed economic growth and thereby failed to generate tax revenues sufficient to reduce the deficit. Furthermore, high interest rates have led to an inflow of investment capital and a high Canadian dollar which, in turn, has hurt exports. Within the first year of operation of the free trade agreement the Canadian dollar rose relative to the American, more than offsetting the gain expected to follow from the elimination of tariffs between the two countries, tariffs which on average were less than 10 per cent (Clarke, 1990).

One important consequence of Ottawa's withdrawal from the social arena is that increased responsibilities have fallen to the provincial level. The traditional radical right model argues that, as government pulls back to its proper and limited role, individuals and local communities will assume responsibility for their own lives. Within a federal system, however, there is an intervening or middle level of analysis, the province or state (Lightman, 1987). Ottawa's cutbacks, ceiling on transfers, and even its withdrawal of support from women's centres were all argued as returning to the provinces their original constitutional responsibilities. The provinces have responded in a variety of ways: the wealthier among them have made up at least some of the missing monies out of their own resources while others have raised provincial income tax levels. In the latter case, the goal of federal deficit reduction is being achieved at the expense of increased provincial deficits: the overall net effect (total federal and provincial deficits combined) is, in principle, unchanged but the burden is simply transferred from a higher level of government to a lower.

The future of the Canadian welfare state

The central preoccupations of Canada's federal government are undoubtedly deficit reduction and federal provincial conflict. The remaining issue for this chapter is whether and in what way these fit into a classic *New Right* conceptual framework.

The complexity of a federal state in crisis has precluded any simple ideological purity at the national level. The more interesting question, however, one which cannot be ultimately answered, is whether deficit reduction is a serious goal in its own right as a way of restoring health to the Canadian economy or whether it simply reflects a means to some broader radical right agenda.

What is clear is that radical right thinking does not command a wide and substantial following among the Canadian public at large: prior to the 1990 budget following a year of saturation media bombardment about the importance of deficit reduction, a major poll did find that a full 80 per cent of a national sample was either 'somewhat concerned' or 'very concerned' about the size of the federal government's deficit. However, when respondents were asked whether government should cut its spending in a variety of enumerated areas — job training; agriculture; economic development in the poorer provinces; social programmes; defence; education and health care; arts and culture — in only two areas — defence and arts — did a majority of respondents endorse cutbacks (Globe and Mail/CBC, 1990). Even within the business community, as we have seen, the goal has not been to cut government spending as an end in itself, but rather to tailor it to serving more narrow and explicit goals of capital accumulation. Thus, the abstract goal of deficit reduction has been detached by substantial elements within both the business community and the public at large from the identification of specific spending cuts. The radical right agenda of cutting spending has been generally, though not universally, rejected when specific areas for cutting must be identified.

If spending cuts are not desired then by definition the only alternative towards deficit reduction involves increased taxation, and it is here of course that Canadian practice and preferences diverge most fundamentally from the radical right's classic agenda. It is perhaps fair to observe since the discrediting of Ronald Reagan's supply-side economics, the radical right has been without a clear and precise economic programme. It has become more a statement of moral views on life: one of these ideological strands is that government should be small and non-intrusive. Such an outcome is unlikely to emerge in Canada.

Part III

Conclusion

9

The radical right and the future of the welfare state

Howard Glennerster

There is no doubt that in Europe, as I write in 1991, the turn of the decade has seen the triumph of the twin ideals of an open society and of the market as a means of allocating resources as against the politically closed and economically centralized systems of the east of Europe. In a way not entirely predicted by Marx, one economic pattern has asserted its functional superiority over another with devastating political consequences.

Nor has the triumph of the private market been confined to Eastern Europe. The United Kingdom has, for the first time for many decades, become an outstanding exporter. Its success in privatizing large slices of its basic industries has become a model for other advanced economies that have large public sectors.

The oil shocks of the 1970s and the consequent recession that followed produced an economic climate that predisposed political systems to consider fundamental reforms. The demographic arithmetic in many countries did the same. Governments faced both declining births among the younger age groups and a growing older age group that will become even more significant in the next century. Virtually all OECD countries succeeded in restraining the growth of social expenditure as a proportion of the GDP after 1975, whatever their mix of private to public services or overall levels of public expenditure (see Tables 9.1, 9.2 and 9.3).

There had been a revival of individualistic philosophy in the previous decade and advances in economic theory challenging Keynesian orthodoxy (Gamble, 1989). In short, the time was ripe for change and

Table 9.1 Social expenditure as a proportion of GDP (percentages)

	1960	1975	1980	1985
Australia	9.5	17.6	17.3	18.4
Austria	17.4	23.4	26.0	28.8
Belgium	n.a.	28.7	33.9	35.8
Canada	11.2	20.1	19.5	22.6
Denmark	9.0	27.1	35.1	33.9
Finland	14.9	21.9	22.9	22.8
France	14.4	26.3	30.9	34.2
Germany	17.1	27.8	26.6	25.8
Greece	n.a.	10.0	12.6	19.5
Ireland	11.3	22.0	23.8	25.6
Italy	13.7	20.6	23.7	26.7
Japan	7.6	13.7	16.1	16.2
Netherlands	12.8	29.3	31.8	30.7
New Zealand	12.7	19.0	22.4	19.8
Norway	11.0	23.2	24.2	23.5
Portugal	n.a.	n.a.	17.3	n.a.
Spain	n.a.	n.a.	15.6	15.2
Sweden	15.6	27.4	33.2	32.0†
Switzerland	8.2	19.0	19.1	20.5†
United Kingdom	12.4	19.6	20.0	20.9
United States	9.9	18.7	18.0	18.2
OECD average*	12.3	21.9	23.3	24.6

*The OECD average figures are the unweighted averages excluding Portugal and Spain for all years and Belgium and Greece for 1960.
†1984.

Source: OECD (1988).

change that favoured radical right ideas. In some countries, too, the radical right was blessed with popular or charismatic politicians to carry the programmes through. It is against that background that the preceding chapters should be viewed. This group of essays has looked at the outcome of these ideas in the welfare field in a group of countries where the impact of radical right ideas was likely to have been greatest. We deliberately left out the Scandinavian countries which have a very different tradition and which have been most resistant to the ideologies we have been discussing. Sweden responded to the recession of the 1980s with an active labour market philosophy that guaranteed workers some kind of job or training if they were out of the active labour force for any significant period. The strong work ethic, which underlies this approach, produced a policy response not that different, in essence, from the workfare programmes advocated in the United

Table 9.2 The growth of real social expenditure (per cent per year)*

	1960–75	1975–80	1980–85
Australia	8.1	1.9	3.9
Austria	3.5	4.8	2.9
Belgium	n.a.	5.0	2.2
Canada	7.6	2.0	4.0
Denmark	8.8	8.4	1.8
Finland	5.6	4.1	1.4
France	7.3	5.5	3.2
Germany	4.8	2.0	0.7
Greece	n.a.	7.6	8.2
Ireland	7.2	5.1	3.5
Italy	5.5	3.9	2.8
Japan	8.5	8.2	3.2
Netherlands	6.4	4.0	2.2
New Zealand	4.0	2.0	1.0
Norway	8.3	6.8	3.8
Spain	n.a.	n.a.	1.1
Sweden	5.9	3.3	0.1†
Switzerland	8.1	1.4	1.8†
United Kingdom	3.9	2.0	1.9
United States	6.5	2.0	2.7
OECD average	6.5‡	4.2	2.6

*Expenditures in constant prices were obtained by deflating current price data by the GDP deflator.
†The '1985' data for Sweden and Switzerland refer to 1984.
‡Belgium, Greece and Spain are not included in the average.

Source: OECD (1988).

States.* Work was preferable to benefits because it gave dignity to the worker and because Sweden's social security and benefits system was based on entitlements earned in the labour market. That would be undermined by massive unemployment. People of both sexes should have equal access to the labour market and hence facilities provided to enable child care to be available for whoever wished to use it. Thus, though it is possible to see similarities in the policy response to that advocated by American authors like Mead (1986), they stem from very different ideological roots. Comparisons with Scandinavia are a well trodden track, however. Our concern has been to look at countries with more divergent traditions where the influence of radical right ideas seemed to be potentially powerful.

*I am indebted to my colleague Jane Lewis's forthcoming work on Sweden for this point.

Table 9.3 Public expenditure on the main social programmes in 1985 (percentage of GDP)

	Education	Health	Pensions	Unemployment
Australia	5.7	4.9	4.9*	1.3
Austria	4.4	5.3	14.5	0.8
Belgium	7.3	5.5	n.a.	n.a.
Canada	5.9	6.4	5.4	3.3
Denmark	7.2	5.2	8.5	3.2
Finland	6.2	5.6	7.1*	0.5*
France	6.1	6.8	12.7	2.8
Germany	4.4	6.4	11.8	1.5
Greece	3.3	4.1	10.7	0.4
Ireland	6.4	6.9	5.4	3.6
Italy	5.9	5.4	15.6	0.8
Japan	4.3	4.8	5.3	0.4
Netherlands	5.6	6.5	10.5	3.3
New Zealand	4.1	4.4	8.1	0.6
Norway	5.6†	6.2	8.0*	0.7*
Portugal	4.4	4.0	7.2	0.3
Spain	2.2	4.3	8.6*	2.1*
Sweden	5.9*	8.5	11.2	0.7
Switzerland	5.5*	5.4	8.1*	0.3
United Kingdom	5.0	5.2	6.7	1.8
United States	5.3	4.4	7.2	0.4
OECD total	5.3	5.6	8.9	1.8

*1984 figures.
†1980 figure.

Source: OECD (1988).

A changed agenda

There can be no doubt that the political agendas in all our case study countries did change in the 1980s and in ways that were not favourable to traditional social policy goals. It is also clear that this had more to do with the fundamental economic changes of the time than it did with the particular set of policy prescriptions that the radical right was advancing. The Canadian case is a good example of this. Even so, the kinds of policy options seriously contemplated were far more diverse in most countries than anything seen for several decades. Moving away from the principle of free education in Israel, making private employers responsible for pensions in Chile and Britain, handing over the National Health Service to private health insurance in Britain, cutting family allowances in Canada, deliberate attempts to widen the distribution of income in all the countries, these were not the stuff of political agendas in the 1960s.

What is interesting to someone from the United Kingdom is how the new agenda was set by ideas emanating from the economics profession and social philosophers from the United States. It was as if the prevailing trade winds had changed. The new world had inherited the Poor Law framework from Britain. It took over and expanded upon the settlement idea in the early twentieth century. The idea of social insurance was directly borrowed from Germany and the British Beveridge Report (1942), setting out a blueprint for social insurance, full employment and a universal set of welfare services was an influential document during the Second World War and after in both Canada and, to a lesser extent, in the United States. In the decades after the Second World War, the flow of social policy ideas was generally from Europe, especially from Britain and Scandinavia, to the group of social policy experts in the United States. It was only when Britain began to experience problems with its own response to racial minority groups that it turned to the United States for ideas. Writers like Marshall, Titmuss, Myrdal and Beveridge are still to be found on social work students' reading lists in the United States as advocates of the pure welfare state philosophy. In contrast, British students read no work from the United States in the 1960s except the Chicago case workers, and about the War on Poverty.

Now all that has changed. The British Conservative Party and its associated think-tanks turned almost exclusively to the United States for its inspiration both for philosophy and for practical policy proposals. Milton Friedman, Robert Nozick, Lawrence Mead, Albert Hirschman, Michael Novak, Nathan Glazer, Alan Enthoven — these are now the diet of Conservative thinkers in the United Kingdom and perforce have become the diet of social policy students too, as they seek to understand what is happening to the social policy debate around them. Much the same might be said about Israel where American literature and ideas from American social science and economics have begun to dominate older traditions. That was most evidently true of Chile where the direct influence of the Chicago School was most evident. The more economically dependent the country has been on the United States, the more the radical right ideas have taken root. West Germany is in a different situation. It was economically robust. Its social science community and conservative social politics was not as dependent on American ideas. As Mangen explains, the Catholic Church's well defined social philosophy and the broadly based institutional framework for social welfare in Germany made it much more resistant to the New Right ideas.

The relative lack of success of the ideology in Canada is therefore an interesting phenomenon as Lightman describes. Canada is economically interdependent with America and many Canadians believe free trade will drag Canada into the social policy, as well as the dominant economic orbit of the United States. Lightman's argument is that the 'chips' and 'chunks' taken out of the Canadian welfare state have been driven by the economic pressures and fiscal imperatives, not by ideological conviction. Despite its proximity, Canada has resisted the trend of ideas in the United States.

Retrenchment

Every country has gone through a period of social policy retrenchment. In almost every OECD country the pace of expansion in social spending has slowed, stabilized or slightly reduced the share of social spending in the GDP (see Tables 9.1, 9.2 and 9.3). After a period of rapid expansion this was a painful enough adjustment, but it was not a process of major dismantling. Health expenditure, which had risen so fast, continued to rise but much nearer to the increase in incomes than had been the case before 1975. Yet this was a phenomenon that affected all health care systems, however they had been financed (OECD, 1987). We see this retrenchment and stabilization rather than significant reduction in the GDP going to social policy in the United States, Britain and West Germany, where the trends in macroeconomic indicators of spending are very similar.

The form the retrenchment has taken is also similar. By and large, the programmes that have suffered are not those from which the broad middle mass of the population draw benefit. They are the programmes that have already been targeted on the poor. This is true of public housing and public assistance programmes in the United States and Britain. The great survivors in both countries were the social security programmes and the health care services that go to either the whole population, as in Britain, or the elderly as is true of medicare in the United States. These increased their share of the GDP. Where services tended to be received by the poor alone they lost out. The 1990 Canadian budget cut core funding to women's groups and natives. In many ways this outcome is precisely what the original advocates of universal welfare would have predicted, as I argued in the chapter on Britain, but it is also consistent with a public choice analysis of the self-interested basis of voting intentions. It is those services that the middle class have most stake in that have survived the best. The stigmatized services targeted on the poor do not have the political clout to resist the pressures of retrenchment.

Extended inequality

The benefit and service side of the equation is only one way to view what has been happening. Perhaps the most decisive changes have been to taxation and the funding of social welfare. High marginal rates of direct or income tax have been reduced in many countries and social security taxes or their equivalent increased. These typically fall more heavily on the poor. Overall, the welfare states that remain are probably now more regressively financed than before but this needs more research in order to be sure. On top of this, and more important in distributional terms, have been the structural changes to Western economies — the decline in well paid jobs in manufacturing industry and the growth of lower paid service sector employment. The stagnation in family income in the United States in the last decade and more is one example (CBO, 1988). The adjusted family income of the richest quintile in the United States rose by 25 per cent between 1973 and 1988 according to the House of Representatives Ways and Means Committee. The average family income only rose by 15 per cent in that decade and a half, but the income of the poorest quintile fell by 9 per cent in the same period while their federal tax rate rose. The poorest are not only relatively but absolutely poorer (*The Economist*, 10 November 1990b). In Britain in 1979, just under 5 million people were living on incomes below 50 per cent of average income — which is one widely used definition of poverty. In 1987 the figure had risen to 10 million. Radical right policies, both economic and social, have been pursued further in Britain than in any other European country. No other European country has had remotely the same rise in poverty levels (see Table 9.4). For the radical right the

Table 9.4 Poverty rates and numbers 1973–7 and 1984–5 (persons)

		Percentage	Numbers (000s)
Belgium	**1976**	7.9	773.3
	1985	7.2	705.9
Denmark	**1977**	12.4	614.9
	1985	14.7	750.0
France	**1975**	19.9	10,173.5
	1985	17.5	9,375.6
West Germany	**1973**	8.8	5,238.2
	1985	8.5	5,026.7
Greece	**1974**	26.6	2,290.2
	1985	24.0	2,280.0
Ireland	**1973**	16.4	486.6
	1985	22.0	770.0
Italy	**1975**	10.6	5,861.1
	1984	11.7	6,678.4
Luxembourg	**1975**	7.9	31.5
	1985	7.9	31.5
Netherlands	**1977**	6.6	898.8
	1985	7.4	1,058.2
Portugal	**1973–4**	23.4	1,793.0
	1985	28.0	2,851.8
Spain	**1973**	20.0	6,794.5
	1985	20.0	7,701.0
United Kingdom	**1975**	6.7	3,624.7
	1985	12.0	6,636.0
Total	**1973–7**	12.8	38,580.3
	1984–5	13.9	43,865.1

Note: Poverty is defined as less than 50 per cent of average equivalent disposable income for each country.

Source: C. Oppenheim, *Poverty the Facts*, Child Poverty Action Group, London, 1990.

widening in the distribution is counted a success. The case against welfare states was precisely that they removed or reduced the effective incentives an economy needs.

Structural change

Even if the level of expenditure on social welfare services remains the same it may be allocated differently. It was part of the radical right's objective to shift the state's role from funder and provider of services, a fused bureaucratic model of service organization, to one in which cash was given to individuals or second best, one in which services were contracted out to private or non-statutory providers of service. Failing that, the preference was for there to be competition between agencies, public and private, for the privilege of providing services. Where possible, prices or charges were to be levied. These last middle-way strategies have been called 'market-type mechanisms' or 'quasi-markets'. As we have seen, various countries have gone in for such adaptations to their delivery systems. There has been a great deal of emphasis in the United States on non-governmental agencies to deliver services to deserving causes and groups such as the disabled or elderly. Non-government agencies were always a part of the Israeli pattern but the range of providers has changed, with the trade union movement ceasing to be the favoured vehicle. The move to private pension arrangements in Chile fits the pattern. Where change has been smaller, in West Germany, the range of non-state providers in the social security system, for example, was always wide. For an international survey, see Bennett (1990).

This strategy does not, of course, reduce the scale of state involvement in the economy. The non-governmental agencies have to be regulated and the contracts may be tighter than was the case with government agencies. Moreover, once spread to groups of this kind the political pressure for more spending may become even greater. If quasi-markets are more efficient and give consumers more choice, they could extend the support service agencies gain from the public. Supporters of social policy have come to accept that some of these quasi-market measures may extend the efficiency and the popularity of the services. A significant change of emphasis is detectable in the response of the British Labour Party, for example, and in the end this may be the most significant of the radical right's achievements!

The battle of ideas

Through the 1980s the radical right undoubtedly had the best tunes. Choice, freedom, markets and competition were things that ordinary people knew and understood in their everyday lives. They did their shopping in the shopping malls. They did their banking or insurance in the carpeted comfort of the private service world. There can be little to surprise us in the idea that public services should mirror these characteristics. Notions of sacrifice and the common weal that held nations together in the post-war world were difficult to sustain. What is far more surprising is the robustness of the social welfare institutions and their scale. What we are perhaps coming to realize as a result of this experience is that social policies have been far more firmly grounded in economic and social theory than many had realized. A survey of the economic literature by Barr (1991) is a good illustration. He surveys recent advances in economic theory and our understanding of the reasons why markets tend to fail or work imperfectly and why governments fail too. The case for public intervention in many areas remains strong. Unemployment insurance is one, health care is another.

If we look around the world to those parts of economies which have remained most resistant to the incursions of the radical right, they are, in large part, those that seem to have a strong economic rationale. One of the most powerful fears within government in Britain that prevented any significant shift to a private insurance model was the evidence that this would bring a cost explosion for all the reasons well known to health economists. It is instructive that in the moves to a free labour market in Eastern Europe one of the top priorities has been the introduction of social security. In West Germany the interdependence of social policy institutions and the market were always well understood.

In Britain there began a revival of interest in ideas of social justice, entitlement and citizenship (Barry, 1989). In the European context, the notion of there being a bundle of citizenship rights and obligations has proven unexpectedly powerful whatever the theoretical problems and debates that surround it.

In his seminal work, *Citizenship and Social Class* (1950), T. H. Marshall tried to impose some order on the events of the post-war period in Britain but also against the broad sweep of history. Marshall's essential argument was that modern industrial societies had not developed as Marx had described as a conflict between classes, rigid class and caste systems, but citizens had won certain basic rights for all people in a nation state. While pre-industrial and early industrial societies could sustain differentiated structures, modern industrial societies required free markets and fluid social structures. Modern nation states could not sustain the allegiance of their populations without granting them in succession first equal and common legal rights like those enshrined in the American Bill of Rights. These freedoms from arbitrary state power distinguished citizens from subjects. These are what philosophers call negative freedoms. The winning of adult suffrage brought political freedom or did so in societies where this suffrage was real, and political institutions were able to function openly. It was stage three that most interested Marshall, for at the time he was writing he saw being created a whole set of social rights and obligations embodied in social legislation passed between 1944 and 1948 in the United Kingdom but with similarities elsewhere. These Acts sought to give citizens the right to a basic standard of education, health, food and shelter. What these Acts of Parliament did was to add positive freedoms to the negative and political freedoms of earlier decades and centuries. As I argued in my chapter on Britain, all are interdependent. The capacity to benefit from the absence of arbitrary state power depends on humans possessing basic living standards. Yet all these rights or entitlements carry obligations, where they can be fulfilled, to participate in the democracy, to obey the law and to contribute to the common purse.

Essentially the radical right have been denying the logic of interdependence between these aspects of freedom. The attempt in the 1980s has been to downgrade or deny the validity of social rights and positive freedoms and insist instead that legal and political rights are fundamental. The history of the 1980s suggests that this is not easy to do. The logic of interdependence is well understood at a basic level and the institutions that embody it are not easy to change, though their precise forms may alter. On the other hand, we have had ample evidence from Eastern Europe that attempts to pursue basic entitlements to the exclusion of legal and political freedom are also doomed.

Western Europe, too, has illustrated the same pattern of development in its move to a form of European citizenship. After the Second World War a European Court and a European Charter of Human Rights was created and has grown in significance in recent years. Then, at a European Community level there has developed a European Parliament, albeit weak but growing in power. More recently, the attempt to create a Community-wide labour and capital market without any barriers has led to calls from the EC Commission for a Social Charter embodying a range of social rights for workers in the new single market. European citizenship seems to be moving down the same path as national citizenship, much to the frustration of many conservatives. Women, too, have criticized the limited notions of citizenship embodied in the 1940s ideal which saw women as dependent citizens, if it saw them at all. Nevertheless, there is a renewed debate and more rigour about the social policy response than in decades past. The outcome may be healthy.

The future

The future, then, seems likely to lie with social institutions that will continue to evolve differently according to the traditions of their past, but are likely to incorporate more elements of choice and competition in fields where this can be accommodated without destroying the rights of common or equal access inherent in the principles of citizenship. As affluence spreads so will more families' capacity to provide for their own shelter and education, for example. The history of housing shows only too well that far from solving the social policy dilemmas it can merely exacerbate them. The more effectively ordinary people can express their preferences not to live next to the poor or the disabled or those with less favoured coloured skins or accents, so cycles set in that are difficult to reverse. The increasing polarization of the housing stock in Europe, despite wide variations in patterns of ownership and forms of social housing, is a case in point. Social policy will increasingly become concerned with the downside of consumer preferences just as environmental policy is increasingly concerned with the unintended consequences of unconstrained private affluence.

At the same time, the world economy and past industrial economic change has forced a wider income distribution in Western societies. Changes in Eastern Europe and Russia may exacerbate this trend to inequality as poor people are free to move. The abandonment of simple Keynesianism has left social policy with far more to do than writers in the 1940s ever envisaged. The interdependence of legal, political and positive freedoms will be more difficult to sustain in the 1990s than at any time since the 1930s.

Bibliography

Aaron, H. (1978) *Poverty and the Professors: The Great Society in Perspective*. Washington, D.C.: Brookings Institution.

Abbott, P. and Wallace, C. (1989) 'The Family', in P. Brown and R. Sparks (Eds) *Beyond Thatcherism*. Milton Keynes: Open University Press, pp. 78–90.

Abramovitz, M. (1982) 'The Conservative Program is a Women's Issue', *Journal of Sociology and Social Welfare*, 9, 399–424.

Abramovitz, M. (1988) 'Why Welfare Reform is a Sham', *The Nation*, 26 September, 236–40.

Ahdut, L. and Sadka, E. (1989) 'Basic Consumer Subsidies and Income Distribution', in Y. Kop (Ed.) *Israel's Social Services: 1988–89*. Jerusalem: Center for Policy Studies.

Alber, J. (1988) 'The West German Welfare State in Transition', in R. Morris (Ed.) *Testing the Limits of Social Welfare*. Hanover: University Press of New England.

Alber, J. (1991) 'Characteristics of the West German Health Care System in Comparative Perspective', in E. Kolinksy (Ed.) *The Federal Republic of Germany*. Oxford: Berg.

Allende, S. (1972) 'Segundo Mensaje Presidencial', in *Allende su pensamiento politico*, Editorial Quimantu eds. Santiago: Quimantu.

Altenstetter, C. (1986) 'Reimbursement Policy of Hospitals in the Federal Republic of Germany', *International Journal of Health Planning and Finance*, 1, 189–211.

Anderson, M. (1980) 'Welfare Reform', in P. Duignan and A. Rabushka (Eds) *The United States in the 1980s*. Stanford, California: Hoover Institution, pp. 160–76.

Angell, A. (1973) *Politics and the Labour Movement in Chile*. London: Oxford University Press.

Ashton, D. N. (1989) 'Unemployment', in P. Brown and R. Sparks (Eds) *Beyond Thatcherism*. Milton Keynes: Open University Press, pp. 17–32.

Atherton, C. (1989) 'The Welfare State: Still on Solid Ground', *Social Service Review*, 63, 167–79.

Auletta, K. (1982) *The Underclass*. New York: Random House.

Baecker, G. and Naegele, G. (1986) 'Wende Ohne Ende — Praxis und Ideologie der Konservativ-rechtsliberalen Sozialpolitik', *Theorie und Praxis der Sozialen Arbeit*, 37, 122–35.

Banting, K. (1987) 'Welfare State and Inequality in the 1980s', *Canadian Review of Sociology and Anthropology*, 24:3, 309–38.

Barker, R. (1978) *Political Ideas in Modern Britain*. London: Methuen.

Baroody, Jr, W. (1982) 'The President's Review', *AEI Annual Report 1981–82*. Washington, D.C.: American Enterprise Institute.

Barr, N. (1991) *Economic Theory and the Welfare State: A Survey and Reinterpretation*, Welfare State Paper No. 54. London: London School of Economics.

Barr, N., Glennerster, H. and LeGrand, J. (1988) *Reform and the National Health Service*. London: Welfare State Paper No. 32 LSE.

Barry, B. (1989) *Theories of Justice*. Oxford: Oxford University Press.

Barry, N. (1987) *The New Right*. London: Croom Helm.

Bell, D. (1960) *The End of Ideology*. New York: Free Press.

Ben-Gurion, D. (1959) 'The Histadrut and the State', in D. Ben-Gurion, *The Sinai Campaign*. Tel Aviv.

Bennett, R. (Ed.) (1990) *Decentralisation, Local Governments and Markets: Towards a Post-welfare Agenda*. Oxford: Clarendon Press.

Berger, B. and Berger, P. (1983) *The War Over the Family*. New York: Anchor.

Berger, P. and Neuhaus, R. (1977) *To Empower People*. Washington, D.C.: American Enterprise Institute.

Berlin, I. (1969) *Four Essays on Liberty*. Oxford: Oxford University Press.

Beveridge Report (1942) *Social Insurance and Allied Services*. London: HMSO.

Blau, J. (1989) 'Theories of the Welfare State', *Social Service Review*, 1, 226–37.

Borzutzky, S. (1982) 'Chilean Politics and Social Security Policies', PhD Dissertation, University of Pittsburgh.

Borzutzky, S. (1990) *From Populism to Neoliberalism: The State, Politics and Social Security Policies in Chile* (manuscript).

Bosanquet, N. (1983) *After the New Right*. London: Heinemann.

Briones, C. (1968) 'Antecedentes basicos y analisis del estado actual de la seguridad social en Chile', *Seguridad Social*, 98, 13.

Bruce, M. (1961) *The Coming of the Welfare State*. London: Batsford.

Bruce, S. (1988) *The Rise and Fall of the New Christian Right*. Oxford: Clarendon Press.

Brunner, J. and Garcia, E. (1981) 'Chile: Un nuevo paisaje cultural', *Mensaje*, 302, 487–94, Valdés, J. G., op cit., Ch. 1.

Brunner, J. J. (1981) *La cultura autoritaria en Chile*. Santiago: FLACSO.

Buchanan, J. (1975) *The Limits of Liberty: Between Anarchy and Leviathan*. Chicago: University of Chicago Press.

Buchanan, J. and Tullock, G. (1962) *The Calculus of Consent*. Ann Arbor: University of Michigan Press.

Buchbinder, H. (1981) 'Inequality and Social Services', in A. Moscovitch and G. Drover (Eds) *Inequality: Essays on the Political Economy of Social Welfare*. Toronto: University of Toronto Press, pp. 348–69.

Bulmer, S. (Ed.) (1989) *The Changing Agenda of West German Public Policy*. Aldershot: Dartmouth Press.

Bulpitt, J. (1986) 'The Discipline of the New Democracy: Mrs Thatcher's Domestic Statecraft', *Political Studies*, 34(1), 19–39.

Bustos, J. (1946) 'La prevision y la medicina social en Chile', Santiago (mimeo).

Butler, S. and Kondratas, A. (1987) *Out of the Poverty Trap: A Conservative Strategy for Welfare Reform*. New York: The Free Press.

Cahuas, J. (1979) 'The Government Economic Recovery Program', in J. C. Mendez (Ed.) *Chilean Economic Policy*. Santiago: Imprenta Calderon, pp. 157–63.

Campbell, M. (1988) 'Business United in Support for Deal', *Globe and Mail*, 17 November.

Canada (1945) Dominion-Provincial Conference on Reconstruction, *Proposals of the Government of Canada*. Ottawa: Queen's Printer.

Canada, Department of Finance (1984) *A New Direction for Canada: An Agenda for Economic Renewal*. Ottawa: 8 November.

Canovan, M. (1981) *Populism*. London: Junction Books.

Central Bureau of Statistics (1987) *Statistical Abstract of Israel, 1987*. Jerusalem: Central Bureau of Statistics.

Central Statistical Office (Annual) *National Income and Expenditure*. London: HMSO.

Chamberlayne, P. (1991) 'The Mothers' Manifesto and Disputes Over "Muetterlichkeit"', in E. Kolinsky (Ed.) *The Federal Republic of Germany*. Oxford: Berg.

Chandler, R. (1990) 'Robertson Moves to Fill Christian Right Vacuum', *Los Angeles Times*, 15 May.

Clarke, T. (1990) 'The Economic Costs Outweigh the Benefits', *Globe and Mail*, 2 January.

Cloward, R. and Piven, F. (1971) *Regulating the Poor: The Functions of Public Welfare*. New York: Vantage Books.

Cnaan, R. (1985) 'Racial Differences in Social Service Delivery: Jews and Non-Jews in Israel', *Social Development Issues*, 9, 56–74.

Cohen, L. and Lightman, E. (1989) 'Sneaky Tax Grab at Seniors' Incomes', *Globe and Mail*. Toronto: 28 December.

Collins, L. and Lapierre, D. (1982) *O Jerusalem!*. London: Grafton Books.

Comisión de Estudios de la Seguridad Social Chilena (1965) *Informe sobre la reforma de la seguridad social chilena*. Santiago: Editorial Juridica de Chile.

Committee on Ways and Means (1988) *Background Material and Data on Programs Within the Jurisdiction of the Committee on Ways and Means*. Washington, D.C.: US Government Printing Office.

Congressional Budget Office (CBO) (1988) *Trends in Family Income, 1970–86*. Washington, D.C.: US Congress.

Conservative Party (1987) *The Next Moves Forward*. London: Conservative Central Office.

Costabal, M. (1981) 'Efectos economicos de la reforma previsional', *Gestion*, VI: 64, 64.

Coughlin, R. (1980) *Ideology, Public Opinion and Welfare Policy*. Berkeley: Institute of International Studies.

Crozier, M. J., Huntington, S. P. and Watanuki, J. (1975) *The Crisis of Democracy*. New York: New York University Press.

David, M. (1986) 'Moral and Maternal: The Family in the Right', in R. Levitas (Ed.) *The Ideology of the New Right*. Cambridge: Polity Press, pp. 136–68.

Day, P. (1989) 'The New Poor in America: Isolationism in an International Political Economy', *Social Work*, 5, 227–33.

De Castro, S. (1976) El Mercurio, cited by Valdés, op cit., p. 28.

Deacon, B. (1983) *Social Policy and Socialism*. London: Pluto Press.

Department of the Environment. *A New Tax for Local Government: A Consultation Paper*. London: HMSO.

Department of Health (1989) *Working for Patients*, Cm. 555. London: HMSO.

Department of Social Security (1990) *Households Below Average Income: A Statistical Analysis, 1981–1987*. London: HMSO.
Diamond, S. (1989) *Spiritual Warfare: The Politics of the Christian Right*. Boston: South End Press.
Dixon, J. (1981) *The Chinese Welfare System*. New York: Praeger.
Doron, A. (1975) *The Struggle Over National Security in Israel: 1953–1984*. Jerusalem: The Hebrew University of Jerusalem.
Doron, A. (1976) *Cross-National Studies of Social Service Systems — Israel*. Jerusalem: State of Israel, Ministry of Labour and Social Affairs, Division of Research.
Drache, D. (1990) 'Canada–US Free Trade', *The Round Table*, 307, 251–66.
Drover, G. (Ed.) (1988) *Free Trade and Social Policy*. Ottawa: Canadian Council on Social Development.
Eaton, W. (1988) 'Major Welfare Reform Compromise Reached', *Los Angeles Times*, 27 September, 15.
Economist, The (1990a) 'Development Brief: The Human Condition', 26 May, 78–9.
Economist, The (1990b) 'American Survey', 10 November.
Edgar, D. (1986) 'The Free or the Good', in R. Levitas (Ed.) *The Ideology of the New Right*. Cambridge: Polity Press, pp. 55–79.
Eisenstadt, S. (1967) *Israeli Society*. New York: Basic Books.
Enthoven, A. (1985) *Reflections on the Management of the NHS*. London: Nuffield Provincial Hospitals Trust.
Errázuriz, E. (1987) 'Capitalizacion de la deuda externa y desnacionalizacion de la economia', *PET*, Documento de Trabajo, No. 57, pp. 14–20.
Esping-Andersen, G. (1990) *The Three Faces of Welfare Capitalism*. Cambridge: Polity Press.
Esser, J. (1988) '"Symbolic Privatisation": The Politics of Privatisation in West Germany', *West European Politics*, 11, 61–73.
Estes, R. (1984) *The Social Progress of Nations*. New York: Praeger.
Fagan, D. (1990) 'Federal Subsidies to Business Under Gun . . .', *Globe and Mail*, 17 March.
Fisk, R., Kiesling, H. and Muller, T. (1978) *Private Provision of Public Service*. Washington, D.C.: Urban Institute.
Fontaine, A. (1988) *Los economistas v el Presidente Pinochet*. Santiago: Editorial Zig-Zag, p. 18.
Foxley, A. (1981) 'Perspectives economicas', *Mensaje*, 301, 411–15.
Fraser, D. (1973) *The Evolution of the British Welfare State*. London: Macmillan.
Frei, E. (1965) Primer Mensaje Presidencial.
Friedman, M. and Friedman, R. (1988) 'The Tide in the Affairs of Men', in A. Anderson and D. Bark (Eds) *Thinking About America: The United States in the 1990s*. Stanford: Hoover Institution.
Friedrich, O. (1990) 'Freed from Greed?', *Time*, 1 January, 58–60.
Gamble, A. (1989) *Ideas, Interests and Consequences*. London: Institute of Economic Affairs.
Gibbins, R. and Nevitte, N. (1985) 'Canadian Political Ideology: A Comparative Analysis', *Canadian Journal of Political Science*, 18:3, 577–98.
Gilbert, N. (1983) *Capitalism and the Welfare State*. New Haven: Yale University Press.
Gilder, G. (1981) *Wealth and Poverty*. London: Buchan and Enright.
Ginsburg, N. (1979) *Class, Capital and Social Policy*. London: Macmillan.

Glasgow, D. (1981) *The Black Underclass*. New York: Vintage.

Glennerster, H. (1977) 'The Year of the Cuts', in K. Jones, M. Brown and S. Baldwin (Eds) *Year Book of Social Policy 1976*. London: Routledge.

Glennerster, H. (1985) *Paying for Welfare*. Oxford: Basil Blackwell.

Glennerster, H. and Low, W. (1990) 'Education: Does It Add Up?', in J. Hills (Ed.) *The State of Welfare*. Oxford: Oxford University Press.

Glennerster, H., Power, A. and Travers, T. (1990) 'A New Era for Social Policy: A New Enlightenment or a New Leviathan', Welfare State Paper No. 39. London: London School of Economics (forthcoming, *Journal of Social Policy*).

Globe and Mail/CBC (1990) 'News Poll', *Globe and Mail*. Toronto: 2 February.

Goldsmith, M. and Willetts, D. (1988) *Managed Health Care: A New System for a Better Health Service*. London: Centre for Policy Studies.

Gottfried, P. and Fleming, T. (1988) *The Conservative Movement*. Boston: Twayne Publishers.

Gough, I. (1979) *The Political Economy of the Welfare State*. London: Macmillan.

Greene, M. S. (1987) 'Crackdown Vowed on Child Support', *The Washington Post*, 24 January, 9.

Grottian, P. (Ed.) (1988) *Die Wohlfahrtswende: Der Zauber Konservativer Sozialpolitik*. Munich: Beck Verlag.

Gueron, J. (1987) 'Reforming Welfare with Work', Occasional Paper 2. New York: The Ford Foundation.

Hall, P. (1953) *Social Services in Modern England*. London: Routledge and Kegan Paul.

Hall, S. (1983) 'The Great Moving Right Show', in S. Hall and M. Jacques (Eds) *The Politics of Thatcherism*. London: Lawrence and Wishart, pp. 19–39.

Hall, S. (1985) '"Authoritarian Populism": A Reply', *New Left Review*, No. 515, 106–13.

Hardiman, M. and Midgley, J. (1982) *The Social Dimensions of Development: Social Policy and Planning in the Third World*. Chichester: John Wiley and Sons.

Harris, R. and Seldon, A. (1965) *Choice in Welfare*. London: Institute for Economic Affairs.

Harris, R. and Seldon, A. (1979) *Over-ruled on Welfare*. London: Institute for Economic Affairs.

Haug, F. (1986) 'The Women's Movement in West Germany', *New Left Review*, 155, 50–74.

Hayek, F. (1944) *The Road to Serfdom*. London: Routledge and Kegan Paul.

Hayek, F. (1960) *The Constitution of Liberty*. London: Routledge and Kegan Paul.

Hayek, F. (1978) *A Tiger by the Tail*. London: Institute for Economic Affairs.

Heinze, R. and Hinrichs, K. (1986) 'The Institutional Crisis of a Welfare State: The Case of Germany', in E. Oyen (Ed.) *Comparing Welfare States and Their Futures*. Aldershot: Gower.

Hills, J. (1990) *The State of Welfare*. Oxford: Oxford University Press.

Howard, R. (1990) 'Free Trade Opponents Claim 72,000 Jobs Lost . . .', *Globe and Mail*, 3 January.

Institute for Cultural Conservatism (1987) *Cultural Conservatism: Toward a New National Agenda*. Washington, D.C.

Israeli Economist, The (1989a) 'Business Briefs', LXV, February, 14–16.

Israeli Economist, The (1989b) 'Who's Flooding the Market with Rose-Colored Glasses?', LXV, March, 13–16.

Israel. Office of Information (1948) *Declaration of Independence*. Jerusalem.

Jansson, B. (1988) *The Reluctant Welfare State*. Belmont, Ca.: Wadsworth.

Jefet, H. (1954) 'The Social Service in Knesset-Israel', in B. Dinur, A. Tartakover and Y. Letschansky (Eds) *Clal Israel: Chapters in the Sociology of the Jewish People*. Jerusalem: Bialik Institute, pp. 460–64.

Jessop, B., Bonnett, K., Bromley, S. and Ling, T. (1984) 'Authoritarian Populism: Two Nations and Thatcherism', *New Left Review*, 147, 32–60.

Johnson, N. (1987) *The Welfare State in Transition*. Amherst: University of Massachusetts Press.

Jones, H. (1990) *Social Welfare in Third World Development*. London: Macmillan.

Jowell, R., Witherspoon, S. and Brook, L. (1989) *British Social Attitudes: Special International Report*. London: Gower.

Judis, J. (1990a) 'The War at Home', *In These Times*, 12–22, 14 March.

Judis, J. (1990b) 'Crack-Up on the Right', *The American Prospect*, 3, 30–42.

Kaim-Caudle, P. (1973) *Comparative Social Policy and Social Security: A Ten Country Study*. London: Martin Robertson.

Kamerman, S. (1983) 'The Mixed Economy of Welfare', *Social Work*, 28, 5–11.

Karger, H. J. and Stoesz, D. (1990) *American Social Welfare Policy: A Structural Approach*. New York: Longman.

Katz, M. (1986) *In the Shadow of the Poorhouse*. New York: Basic Books.

Katzenstein, P. (1987) *Policy and Politics in West Germany: The Growth of a Semi-Sovereign State*. Philadelphia: Temple University Press.

Kerr, C., Dunlop, J. T., Harbison, F. and Myers, C. A. (1973) *Industrialism and Industrial Man*. Harmondsworth: Penguin.

King, A. (1975) 'Overload: Problems of Governing in the 1970s', *Political Studies*, 23, 284–96.

King, D. (1987) *The New Right*. Chicago: Dorsey.

Kirk, R. (1953) *The Conservative Mind*. Chicago: Henry Regnery & Co.

Kloss, G. (1990) *West Germany: An Introduction*. Basingstoke: Macmillan.

Koelble, T. (1988) 'Challenges to the Trade Unions: The British and West German Cases', *West European Politics*, 11, 92–109.

Kohn, K. (1990) 'Israeli Privatization — Gov't to Investors: It's All For Sale', *The Jerusalem Post*, Jerusalem Post Investment Supplement, 16 March, p. 5.

Kolinsky, E. (Ed.) (1991) *The Federal Republic of Germany*. Oxford: Berg.

Kop, Y. (Ed.) (1988) *Socio-Economic Indicators: Israel 1988*. Jerusalem: Center for Policy Studies.

Kop, Y. (Ed.) (1989) *Israel's Social Services: 1988–89*. Jerusalem: Center for Policy Studies.

Kop, Y., Blankett, J. and Sharon, D. (1988) *Government Social Spending in the 1980s*. Jerusalem: The Center for Social Policy Studies in Israel.

Kotz, D. (1989) 'The Downside of Supply-side', *In These Times*, 6 September, 17.

Kristol, I. (1978) *Two Cheers for Capitalism*. New York: Basic Books.

Krivine, D. (1990) 'Beilin is Anxious to Try the Waters of Privatization', *The Jerusalem Post*, V, 1 June, p. 14.

Krotz, F. (1988) 'Zwischen Ahlen und Wahlen: Konzeptionen Christdemokratischer Sozialpolitik', in P. Grottian (Ed.) *Die Wohlfahrtswende: Der Zauber Konservativer Sozialpolitik*. Munich: Berg Verlag.

Langille, D. (1989) 'The Corporate Agenda for Social Policy', paper presented at 4th National Conference on Social Welfare Policy. Toronto: 24–27 October.

Larrain, Luis (1981) Interview, Santiago.

Lees, D. (1961) *Health Through Choice*. London: Institute for Economic Affairs.

Lehman-Wilzig, S. (1989) 'Israel: At the End of Ideology?', *The Israel Economist*, January, pp. 7–10.

Lekachman, R. (1982) *Greed is not Enough: Reaganomics*. New York: Pantheon.

Lemann, N. (1986) 'The Origins of the Underclass', *Atlantic Monthly*, June–July, 31–68.

Levitas, R. (1986) 'Ideology and the New Right', in R. Levitas (Ed.) *The Ideology of the New Right*. Cambridge: Polity Press, pp. 1–23.

Lightman, E. (1987) 'Welfare Ideologies and Theories of Federalism', *Social Policy and Administration*, 21:1, 15–27.

Lightman, E. and Irving, A. (1991) 'Restructuring Canada's Welfare State', *Journal of Social Policy*, 20:1, 65–86.

Lind, W. and Marshner, W. (1987) *Cultural Conservatism: Toward a New National Agenda*. Washington, D.C.: Free Congress Research and Education Foundation.

Lipkis, G. (1990) 'Immigrants Spell Fiscal Dislocation, Says Bank Report', *The Jerusalem Post*, 8 February, p. 16.

Lipset, M. (1960) *Political Man: The Social Bases of Politics*. New York: Doubleday.

Loney, M. (1986) *The Politics of Greed*. London: Pluto Press.

Loveman, B. (1977) *Struggle in the Countryside: Politics and the Rural Labor in Chile, 1919–1973*. Bloomington: Indiana University Press.

Lucas, N. (1975) *The Modern History of Israel*. New York: Praeger.

Luetke, G. (1988) 'Die Sozialstationen: Qualitativer Umbau Oder Abbau Gesundheitleicher Versorgung?', in P. Grottian (Ed.) *Die Wohlfahrtswende: Der Zauber Konservativer Sozialpolitik*. Munich: Berg Verlag.

MacPherson, S. and Midgley, J. (1987) *Comparative Social Policy and the Third World*. New York: St Martin's Press.

Madison, B. (1968) *Social Welfare in the Soviet Union*. Stanford: Stanford University Press.

Magnusson, W. *et al.* (Eds) (1984) *The New Reality: The Politics of Restraint in British Columbia*. Vancouver: New Star Books.

Malloy, J. (1979) *The Politics of Social Security in Brazil*. Pittsburgh: University of Pittsburgh Press.

Malloy, J. (1989) 'Policy Analysts, Public Policy and Regime Structure in Latin America', *Governance*, 2, 335.

Mangen, S. (1989) 'The Politics of Welfare', in G. Smith, W. Paterson and P. Markl (Eds) *Developments in West German Politics*. Basingstoke: Macmillan.

Mangen, S. (1991) 'The German Social State 1949–1989: A Selective Critique', in E. Kolinsky (Ed.) *The Federal Republic of Germany*. Oxford: Berg.

Mardones, Patricio (1981) Interview.

Marshall, T. (1950) *Citizenship and Social Class*. Cambridge: Cambridge University Press.

Marshall, T. (1963) *Sociology at the Crossroads*. London: Heinemann.

Marshall, T. (1971) 'Value Problems of Welfare Capitalism', *Journal of Social Policy*, 1, 15–32.

Mead, L. (1986) *Beyond Entitlement: The Social Obligations of Citizenship*. New York: Free Press.

Medding, P. (1972) *Mapai in Israel: Political Organization and Government in a New Society*. London: Cambridge University Press.

Mendelson, M. (1987) 'Can We Reform Canada's Income Security System?', in S. Seward (Ed.) *The Future of Social Welfare Systems in Canada and the United Kingdom*. Halifax: Institute for Research on Public Policy, pp. 117–46.

Mesa Lago, C. (1978) *Social Security in Latin America: Pressure Groups, Stratification and Inequality*. Pittsburgh: University of Pittsburgh Press.
Mesa Lago, C. (1985) *El Desarrollo de la Seguridad Social en America Latina*. Santiago: Naciones Unidas.
Meyer, F. S. (1968) 'Principles and Heresies', *National Review*, Vol. 20, 859.
Meyer, J. (Ed.) (1981) *Meeting Human Needs*. Washington, D.C.: American Enterprise Institute.
Midgley, J. (1984) *Social Security, Inequality and the Third World*. Chichester: John Wiley and Sons.
Midgley, J. (1990) 'The New Christian Right, Social Policy and the Welfare State', *Journal of Sociology and Social Welfare*, 18, 89–105.
Minford, P. (1983) *Unemployment: Cause and Cure*. Oxford: Martin Robertson.
Mishra, R. (1977) *Society and Social Policy*. London: Macmillan.
Mishra, R. (1984) *The Welfare State in Crisis*. Brighton: Wheatsheaf.
Mishra, R. (1989) 'Riding the New Wave: Social Work and the Neo-Conservative Challenge', *International Social Work*, 32, 171–82.
Mitchell, M. and Russell, D. (1989) 'Race and Racism', in P. Brown and R. Sparks (Eds) *Beyond Thatcherism*. Milton Keynes: Open University Press, pp. 62–77.
Moran, P. (1985) *Politics and Society in Britain*. London: Macmillan.
Morris, J. O. (1966) *Elites, Intellectuals and Consensus: A Study of the Social Question and the Industrial Relations System in Chile*. Ithaca: Cornell University Press.
Mount, F. (1982) *The Subversive Family: An Alternative History of Love and Marriage*. London: Jonathan Cape.
Moynihan, D. (1987) *Congressional Record*, 15 October, S10401–2.
Murray, C. (1984) *Losing Ground*. New York: Basic Books.
Murray, C. (1990) 'The British Underclass', *The Public Interest*, 99, 4–28.
Murswieck, A. (1985) 'Health Policy-making', in K. Von Beyme and M. Schmidt (Eds) *Policy and Politics in the Federal Republic of Germany*. Aldershot: Gower.
Myrdal, G. (1960) *Beyond the Welfare State*. Newhaven: Yale University Press.
National Council on Welfare (NCW) (1978) *The Refundable Child Tax Credit: What It Is ... How It Works*. Ottawa: Health and Welfare Canada.
National Council on Welfare (NCW) (1989) *Social Policy and the Next Budget*. Ottawa: Health and Welfare Canada.
Navarro, V. (1977) *Social Security and Medicine in the USSR*. New York: Lexington Books.
Niskanen, W. (1971) *Bureaucracy and Representative Government*. Chicago: Aldine-Atherton.
Niskanen, W. (1973) *Bureaucracy: Servant or Master?* London: Institute of Economic Affairs.
Nissen, S. (1990) 'Zwischen Lohnarbeitszentrierter Sozialpolitik und Sozialer Grundsicherung: Sozialpolitische Reformvorschlaege in der Parteipolitischen Diskussion', in G. Vorbruba (Ed.) *Strukturwandel der Sozialpolitik*. Frankfurt: Suhrkamp.
Noeldeke, J. (1990) 'Der Beitrag der Krankenversicherung zur Absicherung des Pflegerisikos', *Theorie und Praxis der Sozialen Arbeit*, 41, 50–5.
Novak, M. (1981) *Toward a Theology of the Corporation*. Washington, D.C.: American Enterprise Institute.
Novak, M. (1987) *The New Consensus on Family and Welfare*. Washington, D.C.: American Enterprise Institute.
Nozick, R. (1974) *Anarchy, State and Utopia*. New York: Basic Books.

O'Connor, J. (1989) 'Welfare Expenditure and Policy Orientation in Canada in Comparative Perspective', *Canadian Review of Sociology and Anthropology*, 26:1, 127–50.

O'Connor, T. (1973) *The Fiscal Crisis of the State*. New York: St Martin's Press.

OECD (1985) *Social Expenditure, 1960–1990*. Paris: OECD.

OECD (1987) *Financing and Delivering Health Care*. Paris: OECD.

OECD (1988) *Aging Populations: Social Policy Implications*. Paris: OECD.

OECD (1989) *Economic Survey: Germany*. Paris: OECD.

Offe, C. (1984) *Contradictions of the Welfare State*. Cambridge: MIT Press.

Olsen, M. (1989) 'How Ideas Affect Societies: Is Britain the Wave of the Future?', *Ideas, Interests and Consequences*. London: Institute of Economic Affairs.

Oppenheim, C. (1990) *Poverty the Facts*. London: CPAG.

Padgett, S. (1989) 'The Party System', in G. Smith, W. Paterson and P. Merkl (Eds) *Developments in West German Politics*. Basingstoke: Macmillan.

Painton, F. and Malkin, L. (1981) 'Reassessing the Welfare State', *Time*, 117, 12 January, 32–3.

Panitch, L. (Ed.) (1977) *The Canadian State: Political Economy and Political Power*. Toronto: University of Toronto Press.

Peacock, A. and Wiseman, S. (1961) *The Growth of Public Expenditure in the United Kingdom*. London: Allen and Unwin.

Pfarr, H. (1988) 'Mutterschaft und Mitleid. Der Zauber Konservativer Frauenpolitik', in P. Grottian (Ed.) *Die Wohlfahrtswende: Der Zauber Konservativer Sozialpolitik*. Munich: Beck Verlag.

Phillips, K. (1990) *The Politics of Rich and Poor*. New York: Random House.

Pilz, F. (1978) *Das Sozialstaatliche System der Bundesrepublik Deutschland*. Paderborn: Schoeningh Verlag.

Piñera, J. Speech (1979) Segundo Simposio Latinoamericano y Europeo de Cooperacion Economico.

Piñera, J. (1980) 'Speece Seminario Sobre Reforma Previsional y Evaluacion del Plan Laboral'. Santiago, 29, 286.

Piñera, J. (1989) 'La Reforma Previsional', *Informe Economico 1976–77*, Colocadora Nacional de Valores, 39–45.

Pinker, R. (1979) *The Idea of Welfare*. London: Heinemann.

Pirie, M. and Butler, E. (1988) *The Health of Nations*. London: Adam Smith Institute.

Pitsula, J. and Rasmussen, K. (1990) *Privatizing a Province: The New Right in Saskatchewan*. Vancouver: New Star Books.

Piven, F. and Cloward, R. (1982) *The New Class War*. New York: Pantheon.

Pizarro, C. (1978) 'El Rol de Los Sindicatos en Chile', *Coleccion Estudios CIEPLAN*, 22.

Plant, R. (1990) 'The New Right and Social Policy: A critique', *Social Policy Review, 1989–90*. Harlow: Longman.

Pruess, W. (1965) *The Labor Movement in Israel: Past and Present*. Jerusalem: Reuben Mass.

Rabushka, A. (1980) 'Tax and Spending Limits', in P. Duignan and A. Rabushka (Eds) *The United States in the 1980s*. Stanford, California: Hoover Institution, pp. 100–26.

Reich, R. (1989) 'As the World Turns', *The New Republic*, 200, 23–28.

Reid, T. (1990) 'Taking an Axe to Social Policy . . .', *Globe and Mail*, 17 March.

Rich, S. (1988) 'Panel Clears Welfare Bill', *The Washington Post*, 14 September.

Riches, G. (1986) *Food Banks and the Welfare Crisis*. Ottawa: Canadian Council on Social Development.

Riches, G. (1990) 'Market Ideology and Welfare Reform: The Breakdown of the Public Safety Net in the New Canada', in I. Taylor (Ed.) *The Social Effects of Free Market Policies*. Hemel Hempstead: Harvester Wheatsheaf.

Richter, E. (1987) 'Subsidiaritaet und Neokonservatismus: Die Trennung von Politischer Herrschaftsbegruendung und Gesellschaftlichem Stufenbau', *Politische Vierteljahresschrift*, 28, 293–314.

Riddell, P. (1983) *The Thatcher Government*. Oxford: Martin Robinson.

Roberts, G. (1989) 'Political Parties and Public Policy', in S. Bulmer (Ed.) *The Changing Agenda of West German Public Policy*. Aldershot: Dartmouth Press.

Robson, W. (1976) *Welfare State and Welfare Society*. London: Allen and Unwin.

Rusher, W. A. (1984) *The Rise of the New Right*. New York: William Morrow & Co.

Savoie, D. (1990) *The Politics of Public Spending in Canada*. Toronto: University of Toronto Press.

Scarpaci, J. (1988) *Primary Medical Care in Chile: Accessibility Under Military Rule*. Pittsburgh: University of Pittsburgh Press.

Schindler, R. (1980) 'Mutual Aid as Mutual Exclusion in the Development of Welfare Services: The Case of Israel', *International Social Work*, 23, 48–52.

Schmitter, P. C. and Lembruch, G. (Eds) (1979) *Trends Towards Corporate Intermediation*. London: Sage.

Schoenberger, K. (1990) 'In Japan's Worst Slum, Angry Underclass Feels a Nation's Prejudice', *Los Angeles Times*, 30 October.

Schultze, C. (1977) *The Public Use of Private Interest*. Washington, D.C.: Brookings Institution.

Scruton, R. (1980) *The Meaning of Conservatism*. Harmondsworth: Penguin.

Seidel, G. (1986) 'Culture, Nation and Race in the British and French New Right', in R. Levitas (Ed.) *The Ideology of the New Right*. Cambridge: Polity Press, pp. 107–35.

Seldon, A. (1960) *Pensions for Prosperity*. London: Institute for Economic Affairs.

Seldon, A. (1986) *The Riddle of the Voucher*. London: Institute for Economic Affairs.

Sen, A. (1990) 'Individual Freedom as a Social Commitment', *New York Review of Books*, 14 June.

Sigmund, P. (1977) *The Overthrow of Allende and the Politics of Chile, 1964–1976*. Pittsburgh: University of Pittsburgh Press.

Slack, K. (1966) *Social Administration and the Citizen*. London: Michael Joseph.

Smith, G. (1989) 'Political Leadership', in Smith, G., Paterson, W. and Merkl, P. (Eds) *Developments in West German Politics*. Basingstoke: Macmillan.

Smith, T. (1979) *The Politics of the Corporate Economy*. Oxford: Martin Robertson.

Social Planning Council of Metropolitan Toronto (1988) *Free Trade and Social Policy: A Policy Paper*. Toronto.

Social Policy Reform Group (SPRG) (1971) *Special Commission on Poverty in Canada*. Ottawa.

Social Policy Reform Group (SPRG) (1988) *Federal Report Card, 1984– 1988: A Review of the Government's Social Policy Record*. Ottawa.

Stallings, B. (1978) *Class Conflict and Economic Development in Chile, 1958–1973*. California: Stanford University Press.

Steinfels, P. (1979) *The Neo-Conservatives*. New York: Simon and Schuster.

Stevenson, G. (1977) 'Federalism and the Political Economy of the Canadian State', in L. Panitch (Ed.) *The Canadian State: Political Economy and Political Power*. Toronto: University of Toronto Press.

Stockman, D. A. (1985) *The Triumph of Politics*. New York: Harper and Row.

Stoesz, D. (1981) 'A Wake for the Welfare State', *Social Service Review*, 55, 398–410.

Stoesz, D. (1986) 'Corporate Welfare: A Third Stage of Welfare in the United States', *Social Work*, 31, 245–9.

Stoesz, D. (1988a) 'A Theory of Social Welfare', *Social Work*, 34, 101–7.

Stoesz, D. (1988b) 'The Functional Concept of Social Welfare', *Social Work*, 33, 58–9.

Superintendencia de Administradoras de Fondos de Pensiones (1987) *Boletin Estadistico Mensual*, 74, 42–3 and 53.

Thane, P. (1982) *The Foundations of the Welfare State*. London: Longman.

Thoenes, P. (1966) *The Elite in the Welfare State*. London: Faber and Faber.

Thompson, F. (1990) *The Cambridge Social History of Britain, 1750–1950 Volume 3*. Cambridge: Cambridge University Press.

Titmuss, R. (1958) *Essays on the Welfare State*. London: Allen and Unwin.

Titmuss, R. (1965) 'Social Welfare and the Art of Giving', in E. Fromm (Ed.) *Socialist Humanism*. New York: Doubleday.

Titmuss, R. (1968) *Commitment to Welfare*. London: Allen and Unwin.

Trattner, W. (1989) *From Poor Law to Welfare State*. New York: Free Press.

Tullock, G. (1976) *The Vote Motive*. London: Institute of Economic Affairs.

United Nations Economic Commission for Latin America and the Caribbean (1969) *El Pensamiento de la CEPAL*. Santiago: Editorial Universitaria.

United Nations Economic Commission for Latin America and the Caribbean (1988) 'Preliminary Overview of the Latin American Economy'.

United States Government (1975) *Covert Action in Chile*. Washington, D.C.: United States Senate, US Government Printing Office.

United States, House of Representatives, Committee on Ways and Means (1990) *Overview of Entitlement Programs*. Washington, D.C.

Valdés, J. G. (1989) *La Escuela de Chicago: Operacion Chile*. Buenos Aires: Ediciones B.

Valenzuela, A. (1978) *Chile: The Breakdown of Democratic Regimes*. Baltimore: John Hopkins University Press.

Vegara, P. (1981) 'Las Transformaciones de las Funciones Economicas del Estado en Chile Bajo el Regimen Militar', in *Coleccion Estudios CIEPLAN*, 5, 128–33.

Viguerie, R. A. (1981) *The New Right: We're Ready to Lead*. Falls Church, VA: The Viguerie Co.

Vobruba, G. (1983) *Politik Mit Dem Wohlfahrtsstaat*. Frankfurt: Suhrkamp.

Vobruba, G. (Ed.) (1990) *Strukturwandel der Sozialpolitik*. Frankfurt: Suhrkamp.

von Beyme, K. and Schmidt, M. (Eds) (1985) *Policy and Politics in the Federal Republic of Germany*. Aldershot: Gower.

von Beyme, K. (1985) 'Policy-making in the Federal Republic of Germany: A Systematic Introduction', in K. von Beyme and M. Schmidt (Eds) *Policy and Politics in the Federal Republic of Germany*. Aldershot: Gower.

Walker, R., Lawson, R. and Townsend, P. (Eds) (1984) *Responses to Poverty: Lessons from Europe*. London: Heinemann.

Walters, V. (1982) 'State, Capital and Labour: The Introduction of Federal-Provincial Insurance for Physician Care in Canada', *Canadian Review of Sociology and Anthropology*, 19:2, 175–92.

Walzer, M. (1986) 'Towards a Theory of Social Assignments', in W. Knowlton and R. Zeckhauser (Eds) *American Society: Public and Private Responses*. Cambridge: Ballinger.

Warnock, J. (1988) *Free Trade and the New Right Agenda*. Vancouver: New Star Books.

Wilensky, H. (1975) *The Welfare State and Equality*. Berkeley: The University of California Press.

Wilensky, H. and Lebeaux, C. (1965) *Industrial Society and Social Welfare*. New York: Free Press.

Wiles, P. (1969) 'A Syndrome not a Doctrine', in G. Ionescu and E. Gellner (Eds) *Populism: Its Meanings and National Characteristics*. London: Weidenfeld and Nicholson, pp. 166–79.

Wilson, W. (1987) *The Truly Disadvantaged*. Chicago: University of Chicago Press.

Wolfe, D. (1984) 'The Rise and Demise of the Keynesian Era in Canada: Economic Policy, 1930–1982', in M. S. Cross and G. S. Kealey (Eds) *Modern Canada, 1930–1980s*. Toronto: McClelland and Stewart, pp. 46–78.

Yonah, Y. (1990) 'How Right-Wing are the Sephardim?', *Tikkun*, 5(3) (May–June), pp. 38–9 and 100–2.

Zapf, W. (1986) 'Development, Structure and Prospects of the German Social State', in R. Rose and R. Shiratori (Eds) *The Welfare State: East and West*. Oxford: Oxford University Press.

Index